Educating Children with Acquired Brain Injury

Educating Children with Acquired Brain Injury

Sue Walker and Beth Wicks

David Fulton Publishers Ltd
The Chiswick Centre, 414 Chiswick High Road, London W4 5TF

www.fultonpublishers.co.uk

First published in Great Britain by David Fulton Publishers 2005

David Fulton Publishers is a division of Granada Learning Limited, part of ITV plc

British Library Cataloguing in Publication Data
A catalogue record for this book is available from the British Library.

ISBN 1-84312-051-8

Typeset by FiSH Books, London
Printed and bound in Great Britain

Contents

Acknowledgements

The authors wish to thank Jonathan Punt MB BS FRCS FRCPCH, Consultant Paediatric Neurosurgeon, for his kind assistance in proof-reading, amending and verifying the information contained in Chapter 2 and the glossary.

Thanks also go to Linda Evans, commissioning editor, and Anne Summers, editorial assistant, at David Fulton Publishers, for their help and patience throughout the writing of this book.

Preface

We have long been conscious of the lack of awareness about the educational needs of children and young people with acquired brain injuries (ABI) in the UK, in spite of the availability of publications in other countries. However, there is now an increasing demand for more information about ABI and the ways in which it affects children's progress and potential in school. This book is produced in response to that.

Acquired brain injury is an overall term used to describe the effects of illness or injury to a person's brain during or after its development. It is much more common than most people realise. In fact, if you are a teacher, it is very likely that you will already have worked with one or more pupils who have this condition. You may not have been aware of this!

The aim of this book is to provide information that will enable the optimum abilities and potential of children with acquired brain injury to be realised in the school environment.

We hope the information in this book will help to broaden the awareness and understanding of issues related to the education of children with ABI, together with practical suggestions for strategies and provision that have been successfully used with them.

Note: Throughout this publication we have used 'he' and 'him' to represent both sexes in order to avoid cumbersome phraseology.

Introduction

BEN'S STORY

Ben was 11 years old when he was hit by a car while out riding his bike. He was taken by ambulance to his local hospital and then transferred to the regional hospital which had more specialist facilities for managing his acquired brain injury. He was in a coma for two weeks. As he regained consciousness he was confused and aggressive but these problems resolved. With a lot of help and therapy in hospital Ben gradually regained his motor and communication skills. He made excellent progress and when he was discharged everyone said what a remarkable recovery he had made. Ben and his parents were very enthusiastic about his return to school and looking forward to the whole family being able to get back to normal. His friends and teachers made a fuss of him at first; they were very relieved to see he had made a complete recovery, and pleased to see him back at school. He just needed to catch up with the work he had missed.

But Ben has changed in a number of ways. It takes him much longer to get things done and he often doesn't finish them. He is easily distracted and has trouble remembering information, even very simple instructions. He seems to forget what his teacher tells him from one minute to the next. He can't always find the words he wants to use and reading is much harder for him than it used to be. He gets easily tired and irritable. His friends are not spending much time with him now; he can't keep up with the things they like to do and talk about, they laugh at his silly comments and behaviour but think he is stupid. They also don't like the way he gets angry; he never used to. Ben's teachers and friends are beginning to think that he is different from the Ben they knew before the accident.

They are finding it difficult to understand all the changes that have happened to him.

What is an acquired brain injury?

Acquired brain injury (ABI) refers to any injury occurring to the brain after birth and the immediate neonatal period. Such injuries may be caused by accidents or from diseases or infections. The term does not include brain injury that is congenital, i.e. present at or before birth, produced by birth trauma, or is degenerative in nature.

Traumatic brain injury (TBI) is an acquired brain injury that is caused by external forces – accidents or other injuries – and **atraumatic** or **non-traumatic brain injury** is caused by illness or infection.

Numbers of children affected

Acquired brain injury (ABI) is known to be the single most common cause of disability in childhood, and is often referred to as the 'silent epidemic' of our times (Powell 1994).

Traumatic brain injury

'There are approximately 1 million patients in the U.K. who present to hospitals each year with head injuries. Almost half are under 16 years old' (Royal College of Surgeons of England 1999). Studies indicate that at least 1 in every 500 children suffers a TBI each year (Fletcher *et al.* 1995), although some studies indicate higher numbers, e.g. the Royal College of Surgeons report quoted above and Sharples *et al.* (1990), suggesting 1 in every 200. Published hospital figures do not include a significant number of injuries that go unreported for a number of reasons. Some children with less severe injuries may not be admitted to hospital, although there is increasing evidence that this does not mean that subsequent school-related problems will not follow (Savage and Wolcott 1995), and some acquired brain injuries may not be recorded if the child has other serious injuries.

Non-traumatic brain injury

Collectively, significant numbers of non-traumatic brain injuries also add to the total number of children affected, although each individual illness or injury cause, e.g. meningitis, near drowning, strokes, complications as a result of surgery, etc., is not common.

Survival from acquired brain injury

Improved emergency response systems and medical advances have greatly increased the survival rate of children who are injured. The majority of children who suffer ABI survive the initial injury or illness and have no subsequent reduction in life expectancy. However, any effects of that injury, caused by damage to the brain, also persist so that children and adults continue to live with these consequences.

Numbers of ABI survivors in schools

The enormity of the problem is a cumulative one. The most important figures to consider are not ones of **incidence** – frequency of occurrence – but **prevalence** – numbers currently affected. There are no accurate figures for this, but if one considers that at least 1 in 500 children under 16 years of age will sustain a TBI *each year* and that this number will be increased by the addition of the accumulated numbers of lower incidence, non-traumatic injuries, it is very clear that it is not a rare condition. It has been estimated that, in terms of TBI alone, 3 per cent of the population will be affected by the time they reach adolescence (Mira *et al.* 1992). Many schools, therefore, are likely to have children who have an acquired brain injury.

CHAPTER 1

Understanding the developing brain

The human brain is quite elegantly the supreme organ of learning. All that a person does, all that a person is, emanates from the brain.

(Savage 1994)

The brain controls every aspect of human life. It is responsible for everything we do and think from basic bodily functions, such as breathing, blood pressure or bowel and bladder control, to the expression of personality, emotions, thoughts and behaviour. It controls our ability to move, sense things, plan and organise, to communicate etc. In short, it controls everything! It is therefore surprising that few of us understand or have been taught much about the brain, the all-important part of our body that enables us to know who we are and what we do.

In order to understand the effects of an injury to the brain, it can be helpful to recognise what the brain does, how it works, and what might have happened when it does not work efficiently.

The following description of the basic structure and function of the brain is presented in a simplistic, non-technical way. This is not meant to trivialise the topic, but to provide an accessible and introductory guide to readers who may not be familiar with this. A comprehensive review of brain functioning and development can be found in Anderson *et al.* (2001).

Structure of the brain

The central nervous system is made up of the brain and the spinal cord. The spinal cord is a bundle of nerves that connects the brain to other parts of the body. It receives signals from all parts of the body and relays information upwards and downwards from the brain. It is protected by a series of doughnut-shaped bones called vertebrae – the vertebral column – which surround the cord. Although the spinal cord is susceptible to damage, the implications of a spinal cord injury are very different from injuries to the brain and are therefore not referred to here.

The brain is a complex structure. The terminology that has evolved to describe it is also complex and most structures have acquired several alternative labels derived from Greek, Latin, English or French.

The brain can be described as having three major parts: the brainstem, the cerebellum and the cerebral cortex. However, although each area has specific functions, they are not distinct or separate working units but an organisation of multiple and interconnected systems that are heavily dependent on each other (see Figure 1.1).

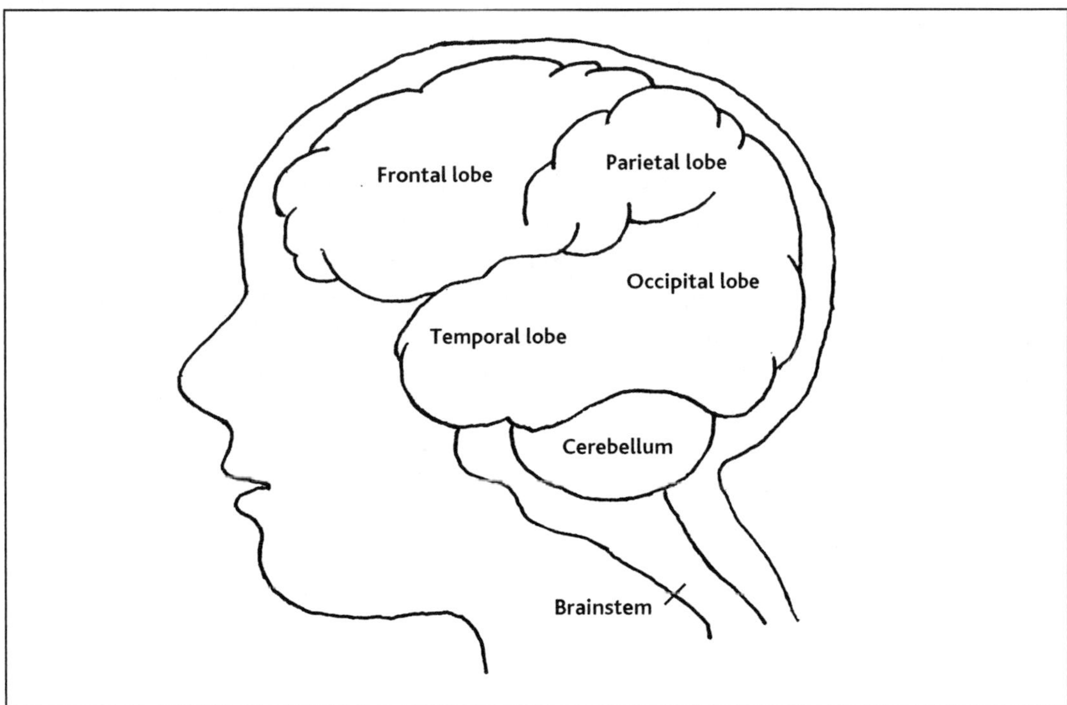

Figure 1.1 Structure of the brain

The brainstem is the lower part of the brain, which is like a thick stalk that tapers into the spinal cord. It is like a telecommunications cable (Powell 1994); a collection of nerves and fibres carrying all messages backwards and forwards between the brain and the rest of the body. The brainstem is responsible for basic bodily functions essential to life such as breathing, heart rate and blood pressure, and plays a vital role in basic attention, arousal and consciousness.

The cerebellum – meaning 'little brain' – is a cauliflower-like structure that sits under the cerebral cortex. It controls and co-ordinates all bodily movement and muscle tone; it develops and stores motor skills that enable us to walk, run, climb, ride bikes, carry out fine motor activities, such as handwriting or using a knife and fork, and many other physical activities. The cerebellum helps control direction, rate, force and smoothness of movement. It is situated just above the brainstem at the back of the brain and is thus relatively well protected from traumatic injury compared to other parts of the brain.

The cerebral cortex is the largest part of the brain, dedicated to the highest levels of thinking, moving and acting, and makes up seven-tenths of the entire nervous system. It is shaped like a walnut: its surface is convoluted with many deep furrows – sulci – and raised surfaces – gyri – enabling increased surface area within the confines of a relatively small skull. Neuroscientists believe that it is the cerebral cortex that sets us apart from all other creatures. The outer lining of the cortex has a greyish appearance and is often referred to as 'grey matter'.

The cerebral cortex is divided into two halves: **the right and left hemispheres**. Although similar in appearance, they have different functions. The left cerebral hemisphere controls the right side of the body and is usually responsible for speech and language functions; the right cerebral hemisphere controls the left side of the body and is usually responsible for processing visual and spatial information and other non-verbal skills.

The differences in capacity to process different types of information in the right and left hemispheres indicates that an injury to the left side of the brain would be more likely to result in language difficulties and/or right-sided problems, while injury to the right side of the brain may produce difficulties with visual perception and/or left-sided problems. However, it is important to note that, although some brain injuries may only affect a specific area or areas, many lead to more widely spread damage (see Chapter 2).

The two hemispheres are linked by bundles of nerve fibres called the corpus callosum, which serve as a bridge or channel of communication between them.

Each hemisphere is further divided into four parts or lobes: occipital, parietal, temporal, and frontal. These are named after the overlying bones on the skull. Each lobe is associated with different aspects of functioning:

- **Occipital lobes**, at the very back of the head, are involved in processing visual information. This includes visual acuity and the way visual information is interpreted, e.g. colour, word or object recognition.
- **Parietal lobes** are located at the back and top of the head, behind the frontal lobes and above the temporal lobes. They are responsible for the processing of information about body sensation – touch, pressure and temperature – as well as the integration of visual and auditory information and an understanding of spatial relationships.
- **Temporal lobes** are located behind the ears and are important for hearing and much of our memories. The left temporal lobe processes receptive language and the right temporal lobe processes musical awareness.

- **Frontal lobes** are located behind the forehead and are the most anterior brain region. They are relatively immature during childhood and develop over an extended period in to late adolescence/early adulthood. They are extremely vulnerable to injury because of the location at the front of the head – it is the most common region of traumatic brain injury. The frontal lobes are responsible for primary motor movements and are very important for the organisation, planning, evaluation, and modulation of behaviour. These behaviours are known as 'executive functions' (see Chapter 4).

Protection of the brain

The brain is protected and nourished in a number of ways:

- **Skull or cranium:** this is the hard bone that surrounds the brain and generally serves to protect it. However, the inner surface of the skull at the forehead has bony ridges, which can result in damage to the soft brain tissue if shaken against it.
- **Meninges:** the brain is covered by three layers of membrane, known collectively as the meninges. The outer one is like a tough plastic sheet and protects the brain from movement, but not if this is excessive or violent.
- **Cerebrospinal fluid (CSF):** a clear watery-like liquid that surrounds and cushions the brain. It is produced in four hollow chambers within the brain called **ventricles** and flows around the brain and spinal cord, acting like a shock absorber.
- **Blood:** provides oxygen and nutrients for the brain; a blood-brain barrier filters the blood and provides some protection to the brain from any chemicals in the blood that could be toxic.

Brain development

Growth before birth

Initially, the human embryo consists of only a few primitive cells, which develop into all the body's vital organs. The brain starts to be identifiable as a collection of cells in the upper part of the embryo when a foetus is three weeks old. By the first nine weeks of foetal development the brain has already taken on its adult shape, with the typical convolutions – folds – of the cortex. The growth and development of the brain in the womb is more accelerated than any other part of the foetus; a newborn baby's brain is one-third of the adult brain weight, although the baby's overall weight is one-twentieth as heavy as the adult it will become (the average weight of a brain in a newborn baby is 450 g and by adulthood the average weight is 1,400 g). As a result, when babies are born their heads are very large in relation to the rest of their body.

Brain tissue is made up of nerve cells or **neurons** and supporting cells called **glial** – meaning glue – cells. Neurons are different from other cells in the body as they are able to generate pulses of electricity when stimulated. As the brain grows, neurons migrate to various locations. This migration is guided by glial cells, which direct the neurons to their ultimate location. When they reach their destination the cells start to specialise.

Prenatal development is primarily concerned with the structural formation of the central nervous system and is thought to be mainly genetically determined. Interruptions to development during this period, such as trauma or infection, are likely to have a significant impact on cerebral structure.

Growth after birth

A newborn baby's brain has about a hundred billion cells, but they have not yet begun to develop the connections that enable the brain to be an organised and integrated system. These nerve cells or neurons continue to grow, sprouting thin fibres, called **dendrites**, like tentacles or the branches of a tree. These fibres enable cells to receive information in the form of electrical or chemical messages. Each cell also has a single fibre called an **axon**, which transmits messages. The more dendrites a cell has, the more neurons it is connected to and the more quickly the message travels.

Very complex patterns of communication develop as the brain continues to grow throughout childhood. Its development is not rigidly predetermined; it gradually evolves over a lifetime. In contrast to development before birth, postnatal development involves the process of developing and strengthening connections between neurons, which is more susceptible to environmental influences. Brain damage sustained postnatally usually has less impact on overall brain structure, but may interfere with this ongoing elaboration of the central nervous system and the development of interconnections and functional systems within it (Anderson *et al.* 2001), i.e. injury can alter normal developmental progression.

The graph in Figure 1.2 illustrates the ongoing development of the brain throughout infancy, childhood and late teens/early adult years. As illustrated, five peak periods of brain growth have been identified, at approximately:

years 1–6
7–10
11–13
14–17
18–21

The brain develops in an ordered, hierarchical way and different regions of the brain have particular growth periods which occur at different chronological ages, with the frontal regions the last to fully mature. The 'peaks and troughs' reinforce the view that children have growth spurts both physically and mentally.

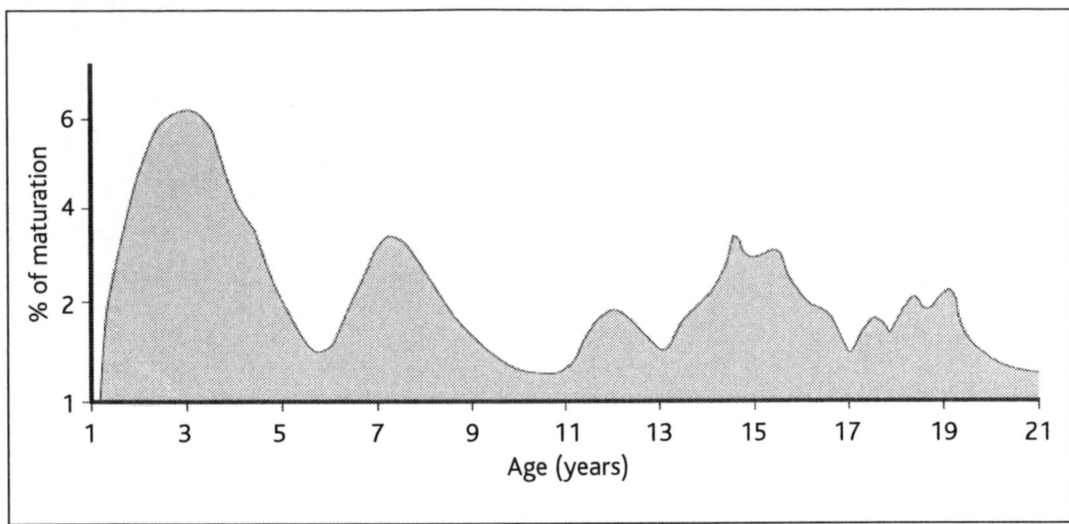

Figure 1.2 Growth of the brain after birth (from Savage 1999; adapted from the original by permission of the author and Lash and Associates Publishing/Training Inc.)

Although the brain's fastest rate of growth is in infancy and early childhood – it reaches about 75% of its adult weight by about the age of three, and 90% by the age of six – it continues to grow and is not fully mature until late adolescence or early adulthood. This protracted period of maturation is unique to humans and reflects the complexity of the mechanisms and the range of developmental processes that evolve. Certain brain areas take many years to mature, or to come 'on-line'.

No two brains are ever exactly the same, even those of genetically identical twins.

CHAPTER 2

What happens in brain injury?

A head injury is usually not just one injury but a series of injuries.

(Powell 1994)

The previous chapter described the complex functions and development of the brain – an amazing 'computer' which exists within the solid 'box' of the skull to maintain the person each of us is and to enable us to live and breathe. However, there are ways in which these delicate systems and functions can be disrupted, with potentially devastating effects. The mechanics and effects of an organic injury to the brain are described below:

Causes

Injury to the brain can occur as a result of a blow or force physically exerted on the body from outside; as a result of an illness or internal imbalance; or as a result of deprivation of an element essential for efficient functioning.

External forces

Penetrating injury

Obvious injuries occur when an object penetrates the skull and can, therefore, damage the delicate brain tissue beneath. This type of injury can be seen, for instance, in gunshot or knife wounds or from falls onto sharp objects. Usually, in such a case, the exact site of the injury and, therefore, the damaged area of the brain is clearly apparent. Except for high-velocity bullet wounds, which cause very severe injury, the damage may be quite localised.

Impact and deceleration injuries

More common are injuries where an object does not actually penetrate the brain itself. This often happens in, for instance, falls, sports injuries, road traffic accidents and assaults. The head may well come into contact with a hard object – the ground or part of a vehicle – which may or may not fracture the skull, but this object does not invade the tissue of the brain. This is called a **closed head injury**. Sometimes part of the skull itself is pushed inwards, which can create an **open head injury** with a depressed skull fracture. The **depressed skull fragments** may tear the brain.

Sometimes there is little or no obvious damage to the outside of the head or skull, but the damage is caused by the fact that the brain has been violently shaken and possibly twisted. It will also then have struck the inside of the skull with force and may have rebounded from back to front. This can happen in road traffic accidents, when the person is being propelled forwards at speed but the body then stops abruptly, and can also be seen as a result of babies being shaken. When an initial site of injury is to one side of the brain, but it then rebounds and is injured by an additional, corresponding impact to the opposite side, this is called **contrecoup injury**.

Other injuries

Any injuries that restrict available oxygen to the brain can result in damage. For instance, children who have nearly drowned in pools or ponds or who have choked may recover but have sustained damage. Similar results are seen from deliberate or accidental hanging or other types of asphyxiation. Soon after cells in the brain are deprived of oxygen, they will die.

Illness

Infections of the brain and surrounding tissue

Meningitis most often affects children and young adults and is a viral or bacterial infection that causes inflammation of the outer membranes covering the brain and spinal cord, the **meninges**. Survivors of this illness can be left with damage to specific aspects of brain function, including deafness.

Encephalitis is the result of infection that causes inflammation throughout the brain itself, not just the meninges. Many different viruses can be responsible for causing this illness, including ones commonly seen in childhood, such as measles, rubella or chicken pox. No one fully understands why, in certain rare cases, these viruses affect the brain, or provoke it to respond with what may be an allergic reaction. Survivors can be left with minor or major deficits in function, either in focal or diffuse parts of the brain.

There is a range of rare conditions, known as **encephalopathies**, that affect the brain in a similar way, but are of a non-infectious origin. These are provoked by occurrences such as a high level of lead ingested into the body; drug intoxication; liver failure; raised blood pressure; or burns.

Tumours, cysts and abscesses

Tumours can develop in children of any age. The brain is the commonest site for cancer in childhood apart from leukaemia – cancer of the blood-forming cells. Tumours are sometimes very small and slow growing, but sometimes develop into extremely large masses at an alarming rate. Regardless of whether these are malignant – cancerous – or benign growths, the fact that they develop within the skull or the brain itself, compressing and invading other tissue and taking up space and blood supply, can cause damage to surrounding areas. Tumours in certain areas can also affect hormonal and chemical balances, further impairing brain function.

Cysts or **abscesses** can form in the brain or originate in areas close to the brain, such as an infected sinus. These are space occupying and can physically damage the brain as a result of their size or cause a source of further infection in the brain itself. These can be fatal if not drained and treated.

On occasions, vital surgery to remove such growths may, in itself, cause some unavoidable damage to the brain. Some treatments, such as radiotherapy, may also cause secondary damage and it is for this reason that this treatment is not used on the brains of very young children. Although irradiation is mainly used to treat illness affecting the brain itself, children suffering from leukaemia may also receive radiotherapy to a specific area of the brain.

Haemorrhage, thrombosis and hydrocephalus

These can all be caused by abnormalities or malformations within the structures of the brain and its blood supply.

The result of haemorrhage – bleeding from a ruptured blood vessel – and thrombosis – a clot in a blood vessel – is a stroke and is well known to us as something that affects the middle aged and elderly. However, this restriction of blood supply, and therefore oxygen, to a particular part of the brain can occur in children as well as in adults. A thrombosis or haemorrhage may result from a number of causes, but there are a small number of children who have one or a number of malformations of small areas of artery walls within the brain. These are called **aneurysms**. These may cause the artery to rupture suddenly and result in bleeding into or next to the brain. There are other vascular malformations that can damage the brain by bleeding or by enlarging to a size whereupon they 'steal' blood nutrients from surrounding areas. They may become very large. These are called **arteriovenous malformations** or **angiomas**.

Any obstruction to the flow of fluid that circulates around the brain and spinal cord – this is called **cerebrospinal fluid** or **CSF** – can cause a build-up of this fluid within the ventricles of the brain, known as hydrocephalus. This can be a secondary result of illness or injury, but can also result from congenital malformation. This increased level of fluid, and therefore pressure, can cause damage to the delicate tissue of the brain. Traditionally, this has been treated by inserting a fine tube from a ventricle of the brain to the abdominal cavity to allow excess fluid to drain away. This is called a **ventriculo-peritoneal** or **VP shunt**. Sometimes the other end of the tube leads to the chest, rather than the abdominal cavity. Recently developed techniques that can be used in some cases involve the insertion of 'drainage' holes in strategic points at the base of a ventricle using an endoscope. This may avoid the need for a shunt. Hydrocephalus may be associated with injury to the brain, either because of the underlying cause of the hydrocephalus, or because of pressure on the developing brain, or even as a result of complications of the treatment, especially infections in shunts.

Other illnesses affecting brain function

A range of other illnesses may, on rare occasions, affect the supply of blood or oxygen to the brain or disrupt the delicate chemical balance of the body, thus causing damage to areas of the brain. For instance, such injury is occasionally seen: after coma induced by illnesses such as diabetes; after continuous uncontrolled epileptic seizures – **status epilepticus**; after a severe asthma attack; or following illnesses causing heart failure.

Degenerative diseases

There is a range of degenerative neurological illnesses that, although rare in childhood, are characterised by the continuing progression of the symptoms. These illnesses include degeneration of the nerve cells and their fibres; inherited or inborn chemical disorders; Creutzfeldt-Jakob disease; those provoked by reaction to vaccine – although this is controversial; and other rare neurological syndromes. It is not proposed to address these here as the purpose of this book is to consider the educational needs of children and young people who have recovered from the acute stage of illness or injury and are left with a non-progressive, acquired injury to the brain

Effects

Having separately considered the varied causes of injury to the brain, the effects of these will now be described. Clearly, there will be differences between injuries as a result of a variety of causes and, of course, each individual case is unique and inherently different. However, these will be explained in general terms as this is not a medical textbook and is intended to provide background information on acquired brain injury for those involved with a child's education.

Medical professionals often refer to primary and secondary injuries – often termed **insults** – to the brain after a trauma. This means injuries that are sustained at the moment when the accident or illness first occurs, i.e. primary injuries, and those that occur after this time, as a secondary result of the initial incident. Doctors are aware that by the time they see the patient, there is nothing that they can do to prevent the primary injuries that have already occurred. Their efforts, therefore, are focused on minimising the effects of these and, as far as possible, preventing the occurrence or severity of secondary insults.

The primary effects of brain injury

Primary insults to the brain include physical damage to or destruction of areas of the brain in penetrating injuries. Anything that prevents oxygen from reaching all or part of the brain, e.g. asphyxiation or haemorrhage, also results in the destruction of brain cells – **neurons**. Neurons cannot normally be replaced and the body's ability to create new ones is limited, so this usually represents permanent loss. There have been recent advances in medical science involving experimental treatment with the implantation of stem cells into the brain to provoke regeneration. However, it is not known at present how this may affect treatment in the future. Recent research also indicates that, contrary to previous understanding, there may be some areas of the brain in which new cells can grow (Smith 2002).

Without significant damage to the skull, an injury caused by external forces can produce a variety of immediate results.

Contusion

Contusion is the medical name for bruising and this will occur in brain tissue as in any other. The brain has room to move within the solid box of the skull that encases it and, particularly in the case of road traffic accidents, the brain may collide at speed with the front of the skull and then bounce off against the back. The inside of the skull is ridged and uneven in some places, particularly the frontal regions, and the brain tissue can be bruised or torn by this impact.

Haemorrhage

More significant bleeding, or haemorrhage, can also occur. Unlike bleeding on the outside of the body, blood inside the skull has nowhere to drain and can accumulate as an increasing-sized clot or **haematoma**. This will compress surrounding tissue and increase pressure within the skull unless it is removed. Surgeons use different terminology to describe a haematoma depending on its location: intracranial – within the skull; extradural – on or over the outermost covering of the brain; subdural – between the outer coverings of the brain; or intracerebral – when bleeding extends into the brain.

Shearing

The brain is made up of many different parts and has a jelly-like consistency with fluid-filled spaces. Structures within the brain are of different sizes and densities. If the brain is shaken inside the skull during an accident these structures will, therefore, move at slightly different speeds. The brain derives from a relatively small base – where the spinal cord enters the skull and joins the brainstem – and it may rotate from this fixed point, as well as moving backwards and forwards inside the skull. As explained in Chapter 1, the brain functions as a result of the vast number of delicate connections within it, from cell to cell and from one area of the brain to another. As the brain is shaken or twisted in this fashion, these connections can break or **shear**.

Connections between brain cells – **axons** – enable communication between cells and, therefore, brain functioning. Severed axons, unlike damaged neurons, can regrow and may effectively reinstate a damaged pathway. However, they do not always regrow correctly or as they were previously and misconnections can be created. When significant shearing has occurred, it is sometimes described as **diffuse axonal injury**.

Coma

This is the term used to describe someone who is not responsive to external stimuli, i.e. not conscious or aware. Medical professionals use something called the **Glasgow Coma Scale (GCS)** whereby responses are scored up to a maximum of 15, i.e. fully conscious and alert, to measure the depth and duration of reduced consciousness. However, this can be difficult to use accurately for very young children, who have not yet developed speech and language function.

Concussion

This is a term that describes a temporary loss of consciousness after a brain injury. Previously it was thought that a mild concussion caused no lasting effects, but evidence of damage to delicate connections or from contusions has now been recognised (see Chapter 13).

Doctors will usually use a brain scan to assess the primary injury caused to the brain. This may be a **CT** (computerised tomography) scan or the more sensitive **MRI** (magnetic resonance imaging) scan. Scans are frequently repeated to assess secondary injuries.

The secondary effects of brain injury

Hypoxia

Recently damaged brain tissue is very sensitive to the effects of lack of oxygen – hypoxia. This may come about because the child's airway is blocked or if the child has very low blood pressure because of blood loss from other injuries – 'shock'. It is now thought that babies who are the victims of inflicted shaking-impact injury suffer brain damage from hypoxia resulting from impairment of the part of the brain that controls breathing and circulation.

Haemorrhage

It is possible that first or further haemorrhage can occur some time after the initial injury. This is a major reason why those attending hospital following a head injury, who seem well and are allowed home, are given advice to return immediately at the onset of specific symptoms. Untreated cerebral haemorrhage is very serious and possibly life threatening.

Oedema

Oedema is an excessive accumulation of fluid within tissue. We all know that if you injure your ankle, it will often begin to swell some time later. This causes no particular additional complications and can be rested until the swelling subsides. However, swelling within the fixed space of the skull is a very different matter. If the whole brain swells, pressure builds up within the skull and the brain itself can suffer further damage, possibly to a fatal extent. If part of the brain swells, damage also occurs as it increasingly compresses the remainder, which can destroy cells or cause further shearing injuries. Such swelling can be provoked by both injuries and illnesses.

One of the main tasks for doctors immediately following a significant brain injury or the onset of a neurological illness is to monitor and attempt to control the pressure inside the skull. **Raised intracranial pressure** is a major cause of secondary brain damage and one reason why some patients die subsequent to the initial injury or onset of illness. The fact that doctors are more able to control this now has been a significant contributor towards the greater number of survivors of neurological illness and injury.

Doctors often make a hole in the skull to insert a monitor in order to constantly check this pressure. Following serious brain injury, children are frequently placed on a ventilator so that their oxygen intake can be carefully controlled. If the brain is not fully oxygenated the automatic mechanism that reduces the build-up of fluid can fail very quickly and the brain can start to swell. As the intracranial pressure rises, the blood pressure is reduced, causing less cerebral circulation and, therefore, higher pressure, in a vicious circle of increasing symptoms.

Many acute centres also elect to sedate children with severe brain injuries and to cool their core body temperature. This reduces the metabolic rate and is said to assist in the process of controlling oxygen and carbon dioxide levels and intracranial pressure, although this is considered by some to be controversial.

After any head injury or other brain insult, there is a chemical response that may produce further damage. This can be likened to a chemical 'burn'. It is governed by factors that are genetically determined, and so different people are more or less likely to suffer this type of secondary injury. Some of the genes controlling these mechanisms are now being identified. This may provide new directions for treatments, and may also explain why some patients have worse outcomes than others from apparently similar injuries.

Infection

Following a head injury there is a risk of subsequent secondary infection after the event. This may be meningitis, spread via an open wound in the skull, or could be infection to other parts of the body secondary to intensive initial treatment. Chest infections are not uncommon in children with traumatic brain injuries during the acute stage.

Post-traumatic epilepsy

It is sometimes the case that a person will suffer one or more seizures immediately after an injury to the brain or following the onset of a neurological infection. Seizures in the first few days after an injury may possibly cause further brain damage, but not necessarily. Seizures following traumatic brain injury are not uncommon and may be the only ones that a child suffers. This does not mean that the child has epilepsy or will go on to develop this. However, any person who has suffered a significant injury to the brain is initially under an increased risk of subsequently developing post-traumatic epilepsy. There is a further increased risk for those who have suffered a penetrating injury or a depressed skull fracture, where the outer coverings of the brain have been infiltrated. Epilepsy can develop weeks, months or even years after the original injury, although this risk gradually decreases over time. Eventually, if this has not happened, the child's risk of developing epilepsy returns to that of the normal population.

Some people, for instance some of those who have a relatively early onset of post-traumatic epilepsy after the injury, will recover from this and stop experiencing seizures. However, others will suffer from this permanently. Epilepsy, of course, can usually be controlled by appropriate medication.

Brain damage

Anything that causes an insult to the brain – be it a heavy blow or invasion of an infectious or other organism – can have a dramatic and significant effect on its ability to function normally. Other parts of our bodies, if damaged or infected, will bruise, swell, bleed or become inflamed, but the difference with damage to the brain is that, unlike the situation with bones, skin or muscles:

- our ability to renew brain cells is very limited
- new and renewed connections between cells can be unpredictable
- the brain has such a crucial role with regard to all other physical and cognitive functions (still developing in a child)
- it is hidden away inside the skull – you cannot see damage to a brain!

It is important to put the emotive term 'brain damage' into perspective: any bump on the head could damage or destroy some brain cells. Many of us may have suffered minor cerebral contusions of which we are unaware. With a more significant injury or illness, as we are considering here, the child or young person will have suffered more significant damage to the brain. Unfortunately, the usual perception or understanding of this term has no foundation in these facts and it is often used as synonymous with very significant global intellectual, and possibly physical, impairment. The popular press and film-makers perpetuate this by emphasising the key question on everyone's lips after a significant accident to a loved one: 'Has he got brain damage?' By which they often mean: 'Will he be permanently unresponsive or severely mentally disabled?'

Unfortunately, therefore, people often see this issue as a clear case of two options. The person will either 'recover', i.e. revert completely back to how they were before, or be 'brain damaged', i.e. completely incapacitated. This is very far from the truth and anyone who has a child with an acquired brain injury will assure you that, far from being clearly black and white, the grey area is extensive.

Stages of recovery

In terms of the results of trauma to the brain, there are many medical and rehabilitation models by which severity of injury and recovery are considered and assessed. From the point of view of families and those working with the child in education, we can consider this in three stages. The first is the acute stage, just after the accident or onset of the illness; the second is the initial period of recovery; and the third is from that time onwards.

It is useful to have an awareness of the earlier stages even if you do not encounter the child and his family until later in this process. Understanding of what will have gone before can raise awareness of the issues and help us to understand the child and family in the longer term. It is also important to recognise the third phase of continued recovery in terms of manifestation of deficit and capacity for rehabilitation; the effects of acquired brain injury for the child and his family do not end when he has 'recovered' in medical terms. This is a different beginning.

Acute stage

When a child or young person first suffers an insult to the brain, it is an extremely traumatic time for him and his family. In more minor cases he may have a concussion or be confused and disorientated. If he has been involved in an accident, he may have other injuries as well, such as cuts or broken bones. With more significant brain injuries the child may be unconscious. He may well be sedated and ventilated and it can be difficult to understand the nature of his conscious state when he is being kept under sedation. Parents may have been told that the prognosis for their child is unclear or even bleak.

Once the child has stabilised, if he has been sedated, doctors will allow him to wake up and to breathe for himself, but the priority is to minimise existing damage and to attempt to prevent further damage occurring. If the child is suffering from an illness or infection, treatment for this will start as soon as possible.

This is a very confusing and bewildering time for other members of the family. If the child has been involved in an accident, they or other family members may also have been injured. Parents may be overwhelmed by a variety of emotions, for instance fear or guilt. They will feel frustration that the doctors and nurses cannot accurately predict the outcome at this early stage.

Early recovery

Once the child is out of danger and his condition has been stabilised, the often lengthy process of recovery or rehabilitation can begin.

Children, particularly those who have been in coma for some time, may return to consciousness gradually. They may begin to respond, for instance to voices, and to obey commands, e.g. to move a hand, intermittently. They are not considered to be out of coma until they are responding consistently.

Any inflammation and bruising will take some time to subside. This certainly often does not happen before the child is seen to 'wake up', which is another myth perpetuated by the media. In films we so often see anxious relatives surrounding the person in coma, who may be swathed in bandages and linked to a bank of machinery. Regardless of the length of time that this is supposed to have continued, we witness the moment when they open their eyes, recognise and speak to their loved ones and drop gently off to sleep before waking to resume their normal lives. You will not be surprised to hear that this does not happen in real life!

After a severe injury, the reality is that, at this stage, children – or adults – may not recognise anyone around them; may not be continent; may be unable to speak; and may have no control over their movements. Bruising, inflammation and severed connections are preventing the brain from functioning normally. It may be apparent that the child has either very tight or very floppy muscles – referred to as alteration of **muscle tone** – all over or on one side of the body, preventing movement on that side.

As the child or young person seems gradually to become more awake or more aware, he may seem distressingly agitated or anxious. He may struggle and toss about as if upset or in pain. When he begins to make sounds it may be to cry out or to moan. This is very disconcerting for the family, although the child will not remember this later.

It can be even more worrying for the family when the child begins to speak, as he may appear to have lost his inhibitions and shout out in an embarrassing way. This can include swearing and cursing, with the child having lost all awareness of social rules. He may be disinhibited and throw off his clothing or masturbate publicly.

This can be likened to a major regression, when an older child or young adult behaves like a baby or toddler. It is as if some basic processes and needs continue to function, but without the benefit of refinement and maturation that have previously occurred as the child grew up.

Not only can this be very upsetting for the family, but it can also be very difficult for the child's friends to cope with if they see him in hospital. Teachers frequently visit with groups of children, and it is important to find out what state the injured or ill child is in beforehand to fully inform the other children about what to expect. They may feel embarrassed about talking to the child if he does not seem aware, or unsure how to respond if he is shouting. It is also important to allow these other children time to talk through their feelings afterwards.

It is sometimes suggested that classmates make a tape or video to send to their injured friend to assist with his recovery. This can be done from an early stage and is thought to help, even if the injured child does not seem to be aware enough to be able to see or hear this.

Not all brain-injured children go through this stage. Some may seem to recover to their previous state much more quickly, while others gradually regain awareness in a much quieter fashion, although they may have initial physical difficulties or problems with speech, eating or drinking.

There is frequently a variable length of time, after consciousness is regained, when the child appears to be aware, but it becomes apparent that he has no continuous memory for events. This is referred to as a period of **post-traumatic amnesia (PTA)**. This period of amnesia is 'lost' for ever, and in older children it can be used at any time in the future as a guide to the severity of the initial injury and to the likelihood of future neuropsychological problems.

For those whose early symptoms are severe or seem to indicate hopelessness to family and friends, the future can look very bleak. Often doctors will be reluctant to give a specific prognosis in the early stages because it can be impossible to predict the extent to which a child will recover. However, when the child then does show signs of recovery and of regaining previous functions, initial progress can be quite rapid.

It is very common to see parents' hopes change rapidly and they continually alter their aspirations. When their child initially appears so badly injured, often their only hope is that he will live, regardless of any disability. The often dramatic recovery process injects a gradually increasing level of hope into their minds. 'If only he can live' can quickly change to 'If only he can speak' and, just as rapidly, to 'If only he can walk', as the previous goals are often quite rapidly achieved. Naturally, family and friends then begin to assume that this rate of recovery will continue until the child is totally back to normal. The press, again, fuels this belief as we see dramatic headlines proclaiming 'Miracle recovery!' Certainly, it is miraculous to see the ways in which the brain recovers from a major assault on its function, but this type of rapid early recovery is to be expected and is not unique.

After this very rapid stage of change, progress does slow down and further recovery takes place at a slower rate. Happily some children do recover completely and can be said to be 'back to normal'. Unfortunately, though, the majority of those who have sustained moderate or severe brain injuries, and some of those with mild ones, will continue to experience acquired difficulties which, for many, will be present for the rest of their lives.

Many parents are understandably very anxious to leave hospital with their child and to return to their normal lives. Most are so grateful that their child has survived and is recovering that they do not contemplate significant future problems. A few of these children will transfer to specialist rehabilitation facilities, but these are rare and most will go home and return to school relatively quickly. The third stage of recovery then begins.

Further recovery and rehabilitation

Many parents say that it is not until they have returned home and are attempting to get back to normal that they begin to realise that the effects of their child's injury are still significant. Unfortunately, as time passes, many realise that the child they now have is very different from the one they knew before. This can be a strange and unnerving situation, as so many of these children make good physical recoveries and look just as they did previously. Despite possible early difficulties with speech, this frequently recovers to an adequate conversational level. It is often the case, therefore, that other people do not recognise the differences and presume that the child has recovered, expecting the same behaviour and abilities as before. Relatives, friends, teachers and others make these assumptions and parents can feel very isolated and unsupported when attempting to face a confusing situation. They may be the only ones who realise that they have brought home a changed or different child from the hospital. Children with acquired brain injury often carry no 'badge of disability'.

The reality is that these children have sustained brain damage, however difficult or emotive that term may be. It does not mean that they will necessarily have any physical impairment and it does not mean that, with appropriate support, they will not be able to achieve academically. It does mean that for years after the injury they will still be going through a process of change and development, which may include some recovery of skills affected by the injury. A serious injury to any part of the body will usually require some form of rehabilitation. This also applies to the brain, but this is a much longer process for a child. It is also the case that, unlike a damaged limb that may require physical rehabilitation, damage to the brain causes cognitive difficulties for which the most appropriate rehabilitation is within educational settings.

CHAPTER 3

Why does ABI provoke different special educational needs?

> *Not all have a physical disability and as a result, many pupils with a brain injury are not perceived as being disabled. The interruption and alteration to a normal progression of development may result in preservation of some skills but loss of others, leading to complex and unusual profiles.*
>
> (DfES 2001a)

ABI presents a challenge for schools because the resultant difficulties are not well recognised.

> Everyone thinks that Mark is fine because he looks so good; he is walking and talking and that is all they have the time to see. We seem to be the only ones who understand that he is not the same as he was before his accident. He may look the same on the outside but he is a different person inside. Everything about him – the things he says and does – are nothing like how they were before. That's the hardest thing, knowing that you've got a different child and not being able to talk about it because no one understands. They don't want to know. Your child looks healthy so what are you complaining about? Sometimes I think it's me that is going mad. (Parent of a 12-year-old boy)

There is now overwhelming research to indicate that children and young people with ABI may require some educational approaches that are different from those commonly or traditionally used (e.g. Ylvisaker 1998, Wolcott *et al.* 1995, Savage and Wolcott 1995).

Acquired brain injuries commonly result in diffuse damage and it is often the combination and complexity of this which results in unusual profiles of learning and behaving.

The crucial issue is that the **processes for learning** may be impaired. Regrettably, too many educators focus on what is visible or obvious, and too few make the connection between an ABI and the disruption to the processes that the brain serves. If they do see sudden changes they may not know why they have occurred, and even if they are aware of an earlier injury they may fail to associate current difficulties with a neurological event that happened months or years ago.

Children with ABI may share a number of similar characteristics with other children with learning difficulties, but there are differences that are important to acknowledge because different and/or additional strategies or supports are often required for helping children with ABI learn and behave appropriately in school. Failure to recognise and accommodate the differences can seriously compromise a child's progress, exacerbate existing difficulties and increase the likelihood of secondary learning and/or behaviour problems. Important basic information for school staff to know is how a particular child's needs differ from those of other children.

Children with ABI have different special needs because:

- **They have had a period of 'normal' growth and development.** Injury and subsequent disability occurs suddenly after a period of normal development. They have often had previous successful experiences academically and socially and may remember these very well. Their perceptions of the differences between present and previous abilities and coping with their sudden loss – of anticipated levels of achievement, of activities, of friends, of skill level, of methods of working – can lead to psychosocial problems such as frustration, anger, depression, withdrawal and/or denial.
- **They often maintain a pre-injury self-concept.** Not surprisingly, people with injured brains cannot easily analyse their own dysfunction. They have great difficulties in understanding their brain injury and the changes to their abilities. They see themselves as they were before; they expect to be able to carry out the same social and academic activities as the peers they identified with prior to their injury. Gradual rejection by that peer group and subsequent isolation and loneliness are commonly reported. They may be resistant to different strategies for learning because they are familiar with and wish to use strategies which have been successful for them pre-injury.
- **There are often significant discrepancies in ability levels.** They may retain or recover some skills achieved prior to injury but not regain others, so resulting in very unusual profiles of learning skills. They may retain good abilities related to areas unaffected by the injury, but have lost skills normally required to demonstrate these, e.g. a child may have excellent vocabulary knowledge, but lack organisational skills to formulate expressive language.
- **There are marked contrasts between pre- and post-injury capabilities.** Acquisition of new learning is most problematic. This is a very important feature that creates an unusual profile, which is very different from other children. They may have learnt and retained skills and information acquired prior to injury, which may seem to be inconsistent with their present slow speed of processing information and significant memory difficulties. Children and young people often score at misleadingly high levels on conventional tests of intelligence because of the knowledge and skills learnt prior to injury, so creating an impression of ongoing competence to achieve

academically. They may achieve to age-equivalent levels initially, but as new learning is impaired, they gradually fall behind their peers.

- **They have an academic and behavioural profile that changes frequently**. The rate at which change can occur and the pattern of academic and behavioural functioning over time can be very different from most children with learning disabilities. This is associated, in part, with neurological recovery. There can be unpredictable and uneven recovery or progress both on a day-to-day basis as well as over a longer term. They can seem to be learning rather rapidly at times and yet there are other times when there appears to be a plateau effect. They can 'grow out' of problems as they recover skills or compensate for impaired ones.
- **There may be delayed deficits**. A child's brain is still developing and the impact of damage may become apparent even years after the injury occurred. There may be injury to a part of the brain that is responsible for skills that do not mature until later within the developmental process and therefore age-appropriate skills then fail to develop. It is sometimes not until adolescence that some difficulties manifest themselves when expected abilities to cope with increasing or different academic and social demands are not apparent. Due to the time that has elapsed between the occurrence of the injury and the emerging learning or behavioural difficulties, there is commonly no association made between the current concerns and the ABI.
- **Family members experience an ongoing grieving process**. 'The grieving is complicated because in one sense there has been no loss – the child has lived' (Ylvisaker 1998). Parents mourn the loss of the child they knew. Plans for the future and educational goals that their child's development prior to injury had led them to anticipate may have to be re-evaluated. It can be difficult for others who did not know the child or family prior to injury to appreciate the enormity of the effects; a brain injury to a child is an injury that reverberates throughout the whole family. Making plans and decisions about any special educational arrangements can be confusing and a considerable source of distress and anxiety for parents at a time when they may already be emotionally overloaded.

CHAPTER 4

Most common areas of difficulty provoked by ABI

We can think of our cognitive system as working in much the same way as a very advanced hi-fi system, which comes as a total package but is made up of a variety of individual parts...A head injury is the equivalent of shaking up this very complex delicate hi-fi system; some parts will be damaged, other parts may work perfectly well. It is important to understand which parts are working and which parts are faulty.

(Powell 1994)

Subtle or significant damage can be caused unpredictably to specific or diverse areas of the brain as a result of accident or injury. Small or large groups of neurons may be destroyed, or it may be the all-important connections between them that are damaged. New connections can be created, but these may not be as efficient and may be created at the expense of others. Damage to neurons whose connections were not mature and developed may affect future maturation and skill development. In contrast, some areas of the brain may be unaffected or new connections may be efficiently formed to restore or to provoke efficient development of specific skills.

Every acquired brain injury results in a unique pattern of strengths and weaknesses, which is frequently complex and unusual and which evolves as a child matures. However, there are some skills that are most commonly affected by an acquired brain injury. It is important to have an understanding of these and the ways in which they may be affected by ABI in order to identify or to address them in schools. Difficulties in these areas may be present in any combination – it is unlikely that all will be affected – and within a limitless range of severity.

The following descriptions mainly refer to difficulties that can be provoked by the organic injury, i.e. damage to the brain. The child's reactions to these acquired difficulties can cause additional difficulties that will be discussed separately.

It will be primarily the cognitive impairments that affect a child's learning ability, but physical, sensory, behavioural, social and emotional problems will also impact on curricular access and academic progress. These are, therefore, also addressed here and in Chapters 7 and 8.

Physical and sensory effects

Many children who have an acquired brain injury may appear to make a good physical recovery. Only a small percentage of children are left with obvious motor impairments. Children usually make a faster and greater recovery of physical skills than of other areas of functioning. This can often lead to false assumptions being made; a relatively speedy recovery of obvious gross motor impairment can encourage a belief that recovery of all other functions will be commensurate with the physical gains. However, this is frequently not the case.

There are often less easily observable but ongoing physical deficits, which are by no means inconsequential. Some subtle impairments can have considerable impact on a child's ability to learn and to feel fully accepted and integrated with his peers. There is also no predictable or reliable pattern of recovery. Some functions may return quickly and completely, others may partially recover slowly, while some physical deficits may be permanent.

Essential to addressing motor skill deficits are the assessments and any subsequent intervention and advice from physiotherapists and occupational therapists.

Motor skills

Injury to the parts of the brain that regulate movement, posture and co-ordination result in gross and/or fine motor difficulties. **Gross motor skills** are the large movements which commonly involve the whole body, e.g. running, walking, jumping, throwing, catching, etc. **Fine motor skills** are the smaller movements, mainly of the hands, for activities involving manipulating, pointing or holding objects, e.g. when using a knife and fork, pencil, scissors, etc.

Motor deficits can range in severity. Total paralysis of large muscle groups, such as **quadriplegia** – paralysis in all four limbs – and **hemiplegia** or **hemiparesis** – motor weakness or paralysis on one side of the body – can severely restrict movement and necessitate the use of a wheelchair or other physical aid. Total paralysis affects only very few children after an ABI; the majority recover motor skills to a point where independent functioning can occur.

More subtle difficulties can result in tremors and poor balance, or problems with motor planning, i.e. the ability to select the required movements in a particular sequence, and motor co-ordination. **Ataxia** involves the loss of ability to co-ordinate movements, which can also result in problems with balance and unsteadiness, i.e. shakiness.

Speed of movement and reaction times are commonly much reduced after an ABI, affecting swiftness and co-ordination which may previously have been apparent, for example in sporting activities or playing musical instruments.

Loss of a child's preferred hand function can sometimes result from motor weakness and so it will be necessary to learn to carry out daily tasks mainly using only one hand or with reduced function in a previously dominant one. Handwriting with the non-dominant hand can be difficult, frustrating and time consuming, particularly for older children. Children often continue to have movement in their affected arm and/or hand but may need frequent encouragement to use it. Children may ignore affected limbs and be very reluctant to use them because of deficits in sensory feedback.

Abnormalities of muscle tone commonly occur after ABI. Muscle tone refers to the amount of tension or resistance to movement in a muscle. This enables us to keep our bodies in certain positions and to make smooth co-ordinated movements. The tone changes when movement occurs. For example, to eat with a knife and fork, the biceps muscles on the front of the arm need to shorten – so increasing the tone – at the same time as the triceps muscles on the back of the arm are lengthened – so reducing the tone. To be able to carry out a movement smoothly, the tone in the muscle groups must be co-ordinated. An injured brain may no longer be able to send appropriate messages to each muscle group, so restricting the range and type of movement of body parts and joints.

Sensory impairments

A brain injury can disrupt any part of the sensory system that transmits or processes sensory information – sight, hearing, smell, taste or touch. **Sensory integration** is the combination and interpretation of information from different senses by the brain to provide a multisensory experience.

Problems with **proprioception** are difficulties understanding where limbs are in relation to the rest of the body and the space around.

Sensory systems are interrelated with many parts of the brain, which is why complete loss of function such as total blindness or deafness seldom occurs following ABI, but also why some disturbance is not uncommon. Some sensory problems resolve gradually, others may be permanent. Visual and hearing impairments have more obvious and profound implications for learning and socialising.

Visual difficulties

Following ABI there can be problems with vision, i.e. the ability to see, or visual perception, i.e. the ability to understand what is seen, or both. Problems are not usually the result of damage to the eyes themselves (although of course this can occur) but to the extensive visual system, which is widely spread across the brain, from the eyes themselves along visual pathways to the occipital lobes, which are in the rearmost part of the brain. Consequently, ABI can cause problems associated with:

- **Tracking** – the ability of the eye to move smoothly across a page of print, or to follow a moving object
- **Focus change** – looking quickly from near to distance without any blurring
- **Binocularity** – using information from both eyes in a co-ordinated way to enable depth and accurate movement perception
- **Fixation** – locating and focusing on a series of stationary objects quickly and accurately (e.g. words when reading)
- **Visual fields** – the total area that can be seen without moving the eyes or head
- **Visual acuity** – ability to see at varying distances
- **Visual perception** – how visual information is interpreted in the brain (discussed in more detail in a separate section).

Or, it can provoke:

- **Visual neglect** – neglect or inattention to visual information located on one side of the body. This can occur despite intact vision and is considered an attentional deficit
- **Diplopia** – double vision.

It is very easy for visual disturbances to go undetected, and common for children who experience them to be either unaware of the extent of their visual limitations through adaptation to them, or to try and ignore them. Spectacles may help rectify some but not many visual problems resulting from ABI.

Hearing impairments

These can create a feeling of isolation for a child and may be very difficult to adjust to if there is no previous history of hearing problems. The ability to speak clearly is often retained, especially if expressive language was already well developed prior to injury. However, a child may no longer have the capacity for checking the accuracy of his own speech and speech therapy may be required. Children who can speak clearly and who may have some lip-reading skills can be easily overlooked at school. Assistive devices such as hearing aids can help a child to locate sound and understand the spoken word under certain conditions, but they rarely completely compensate for a hearing loss.

Fatigue and loss of stamina

Problems with fatigue and sleep are a common part of the recovery process immediately following ABI. However, although they often improve over time after the injury, they can continue to be of long-term concern as they interfere with a child's general level of activity and functioning in school. They have a significant impact on learning because they may affect everything a child does and can be a contributory factor in cognitive dysfunction, irritability, depression and anxiety.

Fatigue

This affects all aspects of a child's functioning at school. Energy levels for both mental and physical activity can rapidly decrease and tiredness can overpower much more quickly and extremely than most people experience. This can affect a child's frustration tolerance and his behaviour. Even if there are no obvious physical changes following an ABI, children and adolescents can become easily tired due to the huge effort necessary to carry out tasks that may well have been completed with little or no difficulty prior to injury. Fatigue and sleep disorders are often not well understood and a recommendation for the child to go to bed earlier is not necessarily the answer – if only it could be that simple! Powell (1994) reports individuals with ABI who have used the analogy of a car running out of petrol: 'very suddenly there is no energy in the tank and you have to stop.'

Many family members report fatigue to be one of the most common and longer-term problems after ABI. Fatigue can be either physical or mental but they are closely related and children with ABI frequently experience a combination of both, but not necessarily at the same time. Mental fatigue may result in a child having limited capacity to stay on task in the classroom, without any evidence of physical fatigue. Although a child may be deemed ready to return to school after injury, fatigue often continues to be a limiting factor for the extent to which he is able to actively participate. A huge amount of effort may be necessary to complete the simplest of school tasks. He may have to work much harder to get a fraction of the work done that he achieved prior to his injury. This greater expending of energy then compounds the child's existing difficulties, making everything else so much more effortful.

Indications of fatigue can be manifested in a range of functions, such as:

- deterioration in balance or co-ordination of movements (e.g. walking in a floppy or haphazard way, or dragging a foot)
- deterioration in posture (e.g. may slump across the desk)
- excessive yawning
- complaints of headaches
- inability to attend and concentrate
- difficulty sustaining a level of performance
- reduced output of work and decreased accuracy
- deterioration in behaviour or compliance.

Medication for seizures, pain or other conditions may also have an effect on fatigue and energy levels.

Making allowances for fatigue can be considered disruptive to class activities, and some members of school staff may believe that the behaviour is just laziness. Flexibility and patience is needed! A common approach to managing the flagging competence of a tired child is with encouragement to 'just do a little bit more'. Many children with ABI are frequently not able to summon up additional resources of energy to make this happen and any pressure for continued effort, which they are unable to generate, can have a negative effect on their behaviour.

Sleep disturbance

This also provokes fatigue. Most of us need a good night's sleep in order to function adequately, both physically and psychologically. However, this is often something that is difficult to achieve following an ABI. Sleep is a process that involves multiple parts of the brain. The states of sleep and wakefulness are the products of very finely tuned, interconnected and interdependent systems. Any disruption to these complex anatomical and biochemical systems, which are spread over wide areas of the brain, adversely affects the timing of sleep and the ability to stay awake, to fall asleep or to stay asleep.

Headaches

Headaches are the most frequently reported symptom after an ABI (Clark 1997). They generally resolve with time but it is important to monitor any changes in their severity or frequency and report them to the parents and doctor. Either continuous or intermittent headaches can dramatically affect a child's performance in school tasks and increase irritability. The severity of headaches can be difficult to define, and may be related to one of a number of causes, e.g. fatigue, migraine or tension.

Epilepsy

Seizures occur when the normal functioning of the brain is disrupted by neurons firing in an excessive or disorderly way. Epilepsy refers to a condition marked by recurrent seizures. The majority of children who experience early seizures after a traumatic brain injury do not go on to develop post-traumatic epilepsy. Seizures can occur as complications of any brain injury; they are not a disease in themselves but a symptom of many kinds of disorders or illnesses that can affect the brain, e.g. encephalitis or meningitis (Anderson *et al.* 2001). If there has been any kind of insult to the brain it is therefore important to rule out the presence of a seizure disorder. It is also important to be aware of a wide variation in the manifestations of the disorder. Some seizures may involve jerking of the arms and legs and a loss of consciousness; others may affect involuntary movement of just one or two limbs with no loss of consciousness. Other forms of epilepsy, e.g. absences or complex partial seizures, can be undiagnosed or misdiagnosed. These may involve only momentary loss of consciousness, in which there may be no movement, or slight facial twitching or diminished consciousness with unusual or bizarre behaviour. Diagnosis of epilepsy is clinical and it needs to be based on detailed descriptions of events witnessed by others and experienced by the child before, during and after what may be considered to be a seizure. Detailed information on types and management of epilepsy are available from organisations referred to in the resources section at the back of this book.

Bowel and bladder functions

Bowel and bladder control involves both physical and cognitive skills; it requires an awareness of the subtle physical signs of needing to go to the toilet and the ability to act on the signs (Powell 1994). Acquired brain injury can affect continence in a number of ways, such as in terms of the urgency and frequency with which the child needs to pass a bowel or bladder movement. A medical and behavioural assessment may be required to ascertain the nature of the problem.

Hormonal changes

Although rare, these can occur following an ABI and can result in precocious or delayed puberty, or changes in growth rate. Secondary sexual characteristics may emerge before the normal time and there may be early onset of menstruation or voice change. This can be difficult for children to manage because the physical and emotional changes, and sexual interests and behaviour normally associated with puberty are not only outside the range of experiences of the child's peer group, but considered inappropriate too.

Appetite and weight change

Weight gain or loss may follow acquired brain injury, for one or more of a number of reasons. Dietary intake during the acute stage of any illness is commonly disrupted and swallowing difficulties can also occur. Rapid increase in weight may result from damage to the part of the brain that controls appetite, so reducing the sense of satiation, although this problem is rare. Problems with weight gain are more often associated with motor impairments which restrict movements, resulting in fewer calories being used up. Appetite and weight change can also be related to behavioural or cognitive changes and need to be clinically addressed.

Language and communication

There are many areas of our brains that have developed in order to enable us to process, to formulate and to functionally use language as communication in speech and writing. Although there are well-known, so-called 'language centres' in the brain, quite different areas are involved when we hear, see, think, speak or write words. Foreign languages are processed in a slightly different area of the brain to that which processes a person's mother tongue (Carter 1998).

The range of a child's vocabulary and his use of language are affected by his environment, but speech is part of normal development. The area of the brain primarily responsible for speech is, for most of us, on the left side. Following ABI it is most usually the case that children will retain or regain the ability to formulate basic speech. Superficially their language skills may, therefore, appear to be intact, but this does not mean that all of the more complex language processes are functioning, or will develop, normally.

The other language skills that most of us use for communication – reading and writing – do not develop naturally like speech, but have to be taught. Like speech, they are crucial to academic progress and achievement and the progress that a child has made in the development of these skills prior to an ABI is important. The ability to acquire new learning subsequent to an injury may be impaired.

Language skills are also closely linked with and reliant upon other skills, such as attention and memory. Many communication and language difficulties following acquired brain injury have their basis in specific cognitive impairment. The ability to speak and to 'hold his own' in normal conversation does not mean that the child does not have underlying problems relating to speech and language ability.

Speech

Following an acquired brain injury, a young person may experience any of the following difficulties:

- **Dysphasia** – an impairment of the ability either to produce or to understand speech and language.
- **Dysarthria** – a condition affecting the muscles necessary to produce speech. This can vary considerably in severity from a mild degree of slurring – sometimes only apparent when the child becomes tired – to virtual unintelligibility.
- **Dyspraxia** – can affect other movement functions of the body, but also speech, and is a condition affecting the use of muscles in a co-ordinated, sequential way.
- **Low volume** – Some of these children have a 'weak' voice, only being able to speak relatively quietly, which may be linked to a lengthy period of assisted ventilation – breathing – in hospital.
- **Mild difficulties** – Children whose speech shows improvement over time may be left with some mild difficulties, such as: imprecise articulation; phonatory weakness; hypernasality; impaired prosody – and pitch variation – or difficulties with rate of speech – slow or rapid (Ylvisaker *et al.* 1994).

Oral language

As previously mentioned, superficially the child's use of expressive language may seem unimpaired. Many children who had normal language development prior to their illness or injury recover the ability to form grammatically acceptable sentences and to use everyday language. They often also perform within normal limits in assessments that are formulated for children with developmental language problems. However, they may have difficulties in the areas listed below.

Word finding

This difficulty relates to the ability to recall specific words from memory. Many children learn to mask this in normal speech and become very adept at talking around a subject or contriving to prompt their listener to provide the missing word for them. This also affects written language, but a young person can sometimes avoid specific vocabulary usage in that context. However, when time is limited or specific vocabulary is required – for instance, during examinations – then their difficulty is all too apparent. Problems with word finding are also most pronounced under stress and so the child will be further disadvantaged in, for instance, assessment, interviews or unfamiliar situations.

Organisation

Difficulties with all aspects of organisational ability can be affected by ABI. This can specifically affect expressive language, resulting in rambling, tangential speech and an inability to formulate an argument or to stick to the point.

Information processing

Slowed speeds of information processing are relatively common following ABI and can affect expressive language. Some children need more time to think through what they wish to say but, unfortunately, this is not always possible. If a teacher asks a question of the whole class or group the child with ABI may not be able to respond promptly. An answer may be blurted out minutes later, to the bemusement of peers and staff who have moved on from the previous topic. The child may also have missed much of what has been said in the intervening period while he was still processing the original question and formulating a response.

> Ann was always very slow to respond verbally when she returned to her primary school following a road traffic accident in which she suffered a significant brain injury. There was concern that she was becoming isolated and her peers and all adults in the school were encouraged to speak to her, even just to say hello, when they passed her in school. You could often hear people call out greetings as they rushed past. Unfortunately, by the time Ann managed to respond to these friendly comments, the people who initiated them had long gone and forgotten that they had never received a reply.

Perseveration

This means repetition of the same word, phrase or topic repeatedly and in an inappropriate way, as if they are 'stuck' within a particular thought.

Abstract thought

If a young person's ability to think imaginatively or to consider abstract ideas is impaired, his expressive language may be confined purely to factual information. Young people with acquired brain injuries – particularly with frontal lobe damage – may be very concrete thinkers.

Auditory receptive language

There may be difficulties understanding spoken language. If a child's speed of processing language is slow, much of what is said by others may be missed. This can be particularly apparent during conversations of children and adolescents, who often chat very rapidly. Other factors affecting understanding of language may relate to the following areas.

Vocabulary knowledge

A child's understanding and knowledge of vocabulary normally increases with maturity. As pre-existing knowledge is frequently preserved after an acquired brain injury, tests of receptive vocabulary knowledge relatively soon after such an injury may well show an age-appropriate level. However, as in other areas, failure to acquire new knowledge at an expected rate often provokes a subsequent widening gap between the vocabulary knowledge of the child with ABI and his peers. It is important to differentiate between vocabulary knowledge and access to this, i.e. word finding.

Quantity and complexity

Simple verbal information, or that presented in small amounts, may be understood, but lengthy or more complex communication can present significant difficulty. This also may be affected by the time available to process this and the rate at which it is delivered. A child may be able to understand information presented slowly and clearly, but not when the rate increases.

Higher level language

Children's understanding of language may be unimpaired at a young age, but they may fail to develop the skills necessary to interpret or to understand more complex language forms as they mature. This is frequently related to lack of appropriate executive skill development and retention of a more immature form of concrete thinking. Young people with acquired brain injuries are often unable to understand subtle humour and sarcasm or abstract and indirect meaning. They may fail to understand figures of speech or metaphors. This only becomes significant when their peers develop such skills and when academic work becomes more abstract. When required to respond to questions, they may be able to answer factual ones but not those requiring deductive reasoning.

Written language

It is important to consider the age and ability of the child when he is injured and to take into account his level of literacy ability at that time. A child injured prior to the acquisition of basic literacy skills is likely to have more difficulty acquiring these than is an older child who needs to regain them. However, there may well be difficulties extending skills learnt prior to injury. Some children and young people with ABI have very significant acquired difficulties relating to written language in contrast to their more efficient spoken language ability. Any one or a combination of motor, cognitive or sensory deficits can impact on this. Some common ones include:

- **Fine motor skills.** Impairment of these and visuo-spatial skills will obviously significantly affect the child's ability to make the co-ordinated movements necessary for writing.
- **Organisation**. Impairment of this skill will also impact upon written work. The child whose spoken language is disorganised, rambling or verbose will produce similar written work. He may do well when required to write brief phrases or sentences, but be completely unable to plan or to organise longer or more complex pieces of written work.
- **Spelling**. Spelling problems are not uncommon in children with acquired brain injuries, particularly for those who were injured at a relatively young age, before a sound knowledge base was established. This can relate to problems with auditory discrimination, but also to memory or sequencing skills or to phonological-processing ability.
- **Reading**. Children with ABI commonly experience much greater difficulty understanding that which they read than with actually reading the words. Reading tests that only assess word recognition may therefore indicate scores within average ranges, but this will not reflect an ability to read for meaning. They also sometimes have more difficulty than would be expected locating information when revisiting text. Their approach to this is frequently disorganised and inefficient.

Social communication

This is highlighted with reference to language because of its significance, but is addressed in more detail in Chapter 8. Difficulties can relate to:

- **Peer expectations**. Being party to the fast-moving jargon and abbreviations of teenage interactions is crucial to social acceptability at that age. Young people with ABI may not understand the humour used by their peers – or may misinterpret it and become the butt of jokes themselves – and may take comments very literally, causing them to be seen as either an embarrassment or a source of amusement to their peers.
- **Non-verbal communication**. There may be difficulties picking up cues from other people's body language and facial expressions and in modifying behaviour or actions accordingly.
- **Socially inappropriate language**. Sometimes irrelevant or inappropriate language can cause trouble or embarrassment. They can sometimes learn to use appropriate social communication skills in a given situation by direct instruction, but find it very difficult spontaneously to initiate or to generalise these.
- **Provocative language**. As teenagers, young people with ABI sometimes use language in such a way as to appear to be rude, inappropriate and challenging to authority.

Attention

A common everyday request for children at school is to pay attention, often with the assumption that this skill is within their automatic control. For most children it is, but following even a mild ABI, there are frequently significant difficulties with the control of attentional processes, which can seriously compromise the ability to learn and lead to more generalised deficits in cognitive functioning (Anderson and Pentland 1998). Problems with attention are among the most common cognitive problems associated with ABI. Also, children who experienced attentional difficulties prior to their injury often find that these are magnified.

What is sometimes thought to be a memory problem may, in fact, be due to a problem attending to the initial information. Attention and memory are cognitive processes that are closely interlinked. Attentional skills are also considered to be an important part of the executive system – the range of processes that are responsible for directing behaviour. This underlines the complexity of the interrelationships between all aspects of functioning – e.g. attentional problems may be as a result of reduced hearing or vision – and the need for accurate assessment of perceived difficulties.

Attention is a broad term that refers to the skills necessary to hold information in consciousness, i.e. thoughts, words, events and objects stimulated by the senses. It includes a number of components and complex cognitive processes, which, during a normal course of child development, emerge at different ages and stages.

Components of attention

Arousal

Arousal is the general state of readiness to respond to the environment and is necessary in order to attend and to make purposeful responses.

Sustained attention or vigilance

This is the ability to maintain attention over an extended period of time. It is often referred to as concentration or attention span and incorporates two elements: the ability to concentrate for an amount of time and the ability to maintain consistency of performance during that time. Sustained attention is disrupted if the child cannot continue to focus on a task, even one that he is interested in, or can only focus on one that does not demand a response, such as watching a television programme.

Selective or focused attention

This is the aspect that people usually have in mind when talking about the notion of attention. It refers to the ability to filter out or to ignore distractions while focusing on an activity. A busy classroom has a multitude of potential distractors – a range of sounds, movements, sights, etc. – that can make it difficult for a child whose attentional mechanisms have been disrupted or damaged. He can easily be drawn off task by something irrelevant and no longer has the control to bring the focus of attention back to what he is required to do. Children may also sometimes appear to be attentive, and environmental distractions can be minimal, but following ABI they are often more easily distracted by their own internal thoughts, which they have impaired ability to inhibit. Being hypersensitive to distractions makes working in classrooms where there are different activities going on simultaneously particularly hard for children after ABI; they have difficulties mentally blocking out what they can see and hear close by.

Divided attention

Division of attention refers to the capacity to attend to more than one task, or to multiple components of a task at the same time. A common example is the ability of many children to complete homework at the same time as listening to music or watching television, or the ability to listen to teacher comments or instructions at the same time as continuing with another task. Being able to do more than one thing at once is often taken for granted because many of the everyday skills carried out simultaneously by most people are within their automatic repertoire, e.g. walking at the same time as talking, riding a bike at the same time as watching other traffic and reading road signs. Following an ABI, being able to carry out just one of them can 'use up' all of a child's attentional capacity, so making it impossible for him to do two things at the same time. An important characteristic of attention is its limited capacity; only so much processing activity can take place at any time.

Shifting or alternating attention

This involves being able flexibly to change focus from one task to another, or from one dimension to another within a single task. Daily school life requires the need to change the focus of attention quickly and efficiently, from one activity to another within the same lesson, or from one subject to another. This is another particular aspect of attentional processing which many children with ABI find hard to do. They appear to 'get stuck' on a train of thought and cannot easily make the transition to another topic. Changes to the timetable or routine at short notice can also be difficult for them to manage because a sudden change of plan requires a child to quickly and effortlessly focus attention in a different direction.

Other relevant factors

In the normal course of child development sustained attention matures relatively early, while processes for higher order or more complex skills, such as dividing or alternating attention, usually emerge later in childhood. Problems with these aspects of attention may, therefore, be one of the deficits that children 'grow in to' as they become older, e.g. pupils at Key Stage 4 may be expected to watch a video or listen to a classroom talk at the same time as taking notes, skills which would not be expected of younger children.

Research suggests that ABI does not necessarily affect the whole attentional system, but may only affect one or several components (Fenwick and Anderson 1999). The younger the age of the child at the time of injury, the more likely it is that the skills that are in the process of developing or have not yet developed will be impaired. This helps to explain why children may be able to successfully attend to some tasks but not others.

Capacity to attend also depends on other factors, such as processing demands, motivation, levels of fatigue, etc. Almost all children, even those with marked attentional difficulties, can sustain attention in some situations. However, if an activity holds no interest for him, the child needs to use more effort to concentrate, particularly if there are competing stimuli in which he is interested. What are commonly impaired following ABI are the internal controls to overcome this.

There is research to indicate that the kind of attentional difficulties provoked by ABI may not be the same as the hyperactive type associated with the developmental disorder ADHD – Attention Deficit Hyperactivity Disorder – but there is no evidence to suggest that the kind of strategies suitable for children with attentional problems of a developmental nature are not also beneficial for children with acquired disorders. However, many children who have attentional deficits after ABI are hypo-active, i.e. they have slowed physical and mental agility.

Information processing

Information processing refers to the capacity of the brain for dealing with information and this is reflected in the efficiency, fluency and speed of response. There are two aspects: the speed of response to information, and the amount of information that can be processed at the same time. There is a limit on both of these. Speed of processing information is closely linked to attentional skills, because the speed at which information is processed affects what can be noticed or 'taken in'. Any slowing down of the processes means that there is less capacity to attend.

Systems for processing information can easily become overloaded. This will, to a large extent, depend on the complexity of the information and the demands being made of the child. The problems of processing overload often increase as the child progresses through school and learning becomes more complex and more abstract. The child may be unable to follow lengthy or rapid instructions, and be slow to respond.

Memory

Everything that we know and have learnt throughout our lives is stored in our memory. Without memory we would not be able to use language; to recognise our friends and family; to read or to write; to learn how to cook or to drive a car; to choose what food to eat; or any other of the millions of activities that make up our daily lives. There are significant variations in different people's memory ability.

Acquired brain injury can disrupt memory to a significant and pervasive level, which bears no comparison with the minor difficulties that we all occasionally face when attempting to remember information.

Memory cannot be considered as a single function. To use the analogy of a library, information must be brought in, evaluated, categorised and stored. There must then be a system whereby any single piece of information can be accessed when required. It is also important that information can be cross-referenced. Use of a search engine on the Internet often produces a huge amount of information, almost instantly. Some of those same pieces of information would also be included, but as part of another set, if a different key word was entered. Our own brains are carrying out similar amazing feats all the time!

Different areas of the brain are responsible for the many facets that combine to make up our memory ability. ABI may have affected some areas more than others. It is, therefore, likely that a child with ABI will have specific strengths and weaknesses of memory and in order to understand this, it is necessary to consider some of the different components of memory ability.

There are many different models of memory functioning but, as in the library analogy, most describe three main processes.

Memory processes

1. **Encoding.** This is the term used for 'taking in' information. This may be something that is read, heard, seen or experienced and which is then 'registered' in the brain. A child's ability to do this is closely linked with other factors, particularly attentional ability, which may also be affected following ABI.
2. **Storage.** This is a very complex process by which information is 'filed away' for future reference. There are different 'levels' of storage, for instance on a short- or long-term basis.
3. **Retrieval.** There is no conscious awareness of all the information that is filed away in our brains, so when this is needed, it must be retrieved from storage or transferred to consciousness. It may be possible to retrieve this deliberately (e.g. to remember a fact to answer a quiz question) or automatically (e.g. remembering how to drive without having to think about it). Information can be stored in our memories for a very long time, even throughout our lifetime. However, following an acquired brain injury, young people often cannot remember – retrieve – information in the longer term if they have not practised recalling it soon after they have learnt it and then at subsequent intervals.

Theories of memory

There are many different ways in which we remember or recall information for different purposes.

Working memory

The first 'holding point' for information that is registered in our brains is within what is often termed 'working memory'. This is information held in conscious memory at any one time. The capacity to hold information in this way is very limited, but can be increased slightly if the information is organised or grouped by meaning. Information is not automatically held in working memory and we need to deliberately hold this there while it is sorted or organised. If a teacher gives a child instructions, these are initially held in working memory.

Following an acquired brain injury, children and young people often have impairments of working memory. This may be related to the fact that they have not efficiently attended to the information in the first place, or to the fact that their organisational skills are poor and they cannot efficiently 'manipulate' or sort the information.

Episodic memory

This is from personal experiences or episodes in our lives. These events are not necessarily remembered consciously, but they are retained in memory. They can be termed 'autobiographical' memories. Children with ABI often have difficulties remembering such events and experiences subsequent to their injury.

Procedural memory

This is a series of actions or a 'procedure' that is learnt, usually through practice and repetition, which becomes automatic and which then does not have to be consciously considered. An example of this is the ability to drive a car. Once experienced, people do not consciously consider the learnt, 'mechanical' actions such as changing gear or turning the steering wheel. Young people with ABI often retain an ability to use this type of procedural memory relatively well.

Semantic memory

This is information or knowledge, free of context, which is learnt deliberately. Many young people with ABI have significant difficulty deliberately learning semantic information out of context.

Explicit and implicit memory

Memory can also be classified in terms of deliberate or incidental learning, i.e. information that we make an effort to learn and that which we 'pick up' without realising it. Young children learn a great deal incidentally, through play, and early years teachers are very aware of this. These types of learning may be classified as:

- **Explicit** – referring to the process of consciously learning and remembering information, therefore being aware of having learnt it and how this was done. This can be difficult for young people after ABI.
- **Implicit** – referring to the acquisition of skills or knowledge without consciously learning it.

Sensory modalities

Other factors affecting a person's ability to remember information relate to the sensory modality with which it is initially encoded or 'registered'. Within the population in general, some people remember things that they have seen – **visual memory** – more readily than things that they hear – **auditory memory**. We are often consciously – or sub-consciously – aware of our own preferences and some people, therefore, always like to write down verbal information that they need to remember. Others like to repeat something verbally if they are presented with it in writing. Use of our hands – for instance to write – can also help some people to remember and this is referred to as **motor memory**, e.g. some people recall phone numbers by remembering the pattern of their fingers on the telephone key pad. Specific damage caused by ABI may affect a person's ability to remember information encoded via one of these methods. However, if the young person always preferred to remember information presented visually prior to his injury and this is now a relative weakness, it will be particularly difficult for him to focus more on auditory information, if this has then become a relative strength.

Recall

It is important that information can be efficiently recalled when necessary. This process can also be impaired as a result of acquired brain injury. Our ability to recall or to retrieve information from our memory stores can be a deliberate process, involving a strategic search of our memory stores, or it can be an automatic process, whereby information is produced when required, e.g. vocabulary when speaking or writing. Prompts for deliberate recall are usually of the following types:

- **Free recall.** This is when a person is asked an open-ended question and has to search memory stores independently for the relevant information. Young people with memory impairments following ABI frequently find this very difficult – their retrieval skills are often disorganised and inefficient.
- **Cued recall.** This refers to instances where there is provision of a cue or prompt to help recall information from memory. This may, for instance, be in terms of a 'category' in which to search, or the initial sound of a word, etc. This often assists young people with memory impairments following ABI to retrieve stored information.
- **Recognition.** In this instance, the person is faced with a stimulus to which they can match information from memory. This type of recall is used in multiple-choice formats and is often a relative strength for young people with ABI.

Memory impairments

There are many contributory factors towards efficient memory. Information may not be efficiently encoded – or stored – but, equally, it may be stored but the child cannot retrieve it at all, or cannot do so quickly enough. If all the books in a library were tipped off the shelves and mixed up, it would take some considerable time to find specific information. However, some clues would help, such as the colour of the book's cover, hardback or paperback, large or small and so on.

Generally, lost memory ability cannot be restored – although there is often spontaneous recovery during the early stages after injury – but strategies can be learnt to maximise ability and preserved strengths.

Perception

Perception relates to the way in which we process information that enters the body through one or more of our senses. All information that we receive from our environment must enter our brains via our vision, hearing, taste, touch, or sense of smell.

The development of our ability to understand and to process information from our environment is incremental and increases as we store information from our experiences. Hence, once a child has seen or heard certain things, knowledge regarding these will be stored and linked with future incoming information. Therefore, a child who is familiar with animals would be able to recognise a dog by touching it, even if he had his eyes shut, or by hearing it if he could not see it. As information regarding the sound, touch and appearance of a dog are linked in his memory store, he would also be able to tell you what sound it makes from just looking at it or what it feels like from just hearing it. The more that we experience, the more we are able to interpret from sensory input and, with increasing developmental maturity, the more sophisticated our perceptual skills become. Therefore memory is important to this development, as is language and organisation.

Increasingly, therefore, as children normally develop, perceptual ability becomes more closely linked with and inseparable from other cognitive skills.

As with all other areas of brain functioning, an acquired brain injury can disrupt aspects of perceptual processing. A common acquired impairment is a loss of ability to 'filter' incoming information and to focus on one aspect of this. Hence, it is not uncommon for young people who have suffered an acquired brain injury to find it difficult to cope with environments that are particularly noisy or which include high levels of sensory stimuli. They may become hypersensitive to, for instance, noise or touch, e.g. someone rustling a newspaper, a cat purring or a minor itch. They may become unable to cope with or distinguish between more than one sensation concurrently, e.g. a bright visual display combined with sound. It is as if these incoming stimuli become confused so that the person soon reaches sensory 'overload'.

Visuo-perception

Visuo-perception is the ability to make sense of what is seen. This is not to be confused with vision, which is the ability to see. Impairment of visuo-perception is relatively common following an acquired brain injury. It is also something that can easily be missed or misinterpreted, despite its potentially significant effects on academic progress and potential. There may be alteration to one or more aspects, examples of which are given below.

Form constancy

This is the ability to recognise the actual shape of an object despite variations in the way that it is seen – e.g. a door that is closed, open or viewed from different parts of a room will look different, although the shape of the door itself will not change. The same shape can also be recognised despite being seen in different sizes, colours, etc. – e.g. a circle can be recognised when seen as a dinner plate, a letter 'O', a clock face or a window. If a child has impairment of this ability it may affect many aspects of the curriculum involving visually presented material.

Figure ground perception

This is the ability to recognise shapes or objects as distinct from the background on which they are presented. If his desk is covered in books and papers, a child can usually look across it and pick out a visible item that he is looking for. Normally it is possible to 'filter out' other things within a field of vision and then focus on one specific thing. If a child has impairment of this ability, this may mean that he cannot search for things, cannot recognise one thing among others, or that he cannot play certain sports. It may also mean that he cannot read if there is too much information on the page or if the text is next to or over illustrations.

Position in space

This is the ability to recognise the orientation of an object or shape within 'space', i.e. the immediate environment. If a child sees a drawing on a page, he knows if it is upright or tilted at an angle and can usually tell if something has been placed upside down or back to front. If a child has impairment of this ability, he may be unaware of rotations and reversals. He may have difficulty matching identical shapes that are in the same orientation. This may affect his ability to efficiently recognise letters and numbers and to write these without reversals. It may affect his ability in practical subjects such as Design Technology or Science, as well as in Maths.

Spatial relations

This also refers to the ability to perceive shapes or objects within space but in relation to each other. It is important when deciding what can be fitted onto a page, or how close objects are to each other, or how fast something is moving. If a child has impairment of this ability he may be unable efficiently to copy or create diagrams or illustrations; he may produce untidy work or lack understanding of where to place information on a page. He may start the top of a drawing at the bottom of a page and then wonder why he has run out of paper. He may have difficulty with some sports, bump into people or not seem aware of personal space and he may be unsafe when crossing roads.

Visual closure

This is the ability to 'match' something that can only be seen partially, with knowledge of the whole object and therefore to 'visualise' the whole. From the relevant developmental stage, if a child saw the top of a chair – the rest being hidden under a table – he would still know what it was. If he saw a partially completed drawing of something familiar he would know what it was. Children with impairment of these skills find it very difficult to visualise anything unless they can see the whole. This may affect their ability to draw conclusions from or to interpret any visually presented information, unless this is very explicit.

Executive functioning

Executive functioning is an umbrella term that refers to a range of skills needed to control and monitor all aspects of intentional behaviour. This describes almost all activities in daily home, school and community life; executive processes are required to succeed at any task that is non-routine. Cognitive processes, emotional responses and behavioural actions are all dependent on executive functioning. The term was so devised because it describes a collection of skills similar to those expected of an administrative executive, i.e. someone who makes plans, sets goals, organises ways in which those plans and goals can be achieved, and who is able to monitor and adjust the plans if necessary, apply sound judgement and have a good overall understanding and management of the situation.

There are a number of different regions of the brain that are involved in executive function processes, but the processes are most closely associated with the frontal and prefrontal regions of the brain, which is why executive functioning deficits – or dysexecutive syndrome, as it is also called – have sometimes been referred to as frontal lobe difficulties, although the two are not synonymous. This area of the brain is very vulnerable to damage and so is commonly affected in acquired injury, often with very significant implications for a child's academic, social and emotional functioning.

Children with ABI may, therefore, show difficulties with:

- **Planning and organising:** because their thinking can be disorganised it may be hard for them to identify and arrange the sequence of steps needed to carry out and complete a task (e.g. a child may dive in and start an activity without thinking about logical, sequential steps needed to succeed and then become very confused and frustrated not knowing how to complete it).
- **Initiating and sustaining:** a child may have the knowledge and skills to carry out a task but be unable to get started – to initiate the activity – and to stick with it to completion, unless prompted by others. This can give others the impression that he is apathetic, unmotivated or unresponsive.
- **Goal setting:** this involves thinking about the 'end product' of a task or activity and working on something appropriate or relevant towards its completion. Without a goal in mind, thinking can be disjointed and disorganised (e.g. a young child may want to paint a picture – that, therefore, is his goal – so needs to be aware of the specific and sequential steps to be carried out to achieve it).
- **Inhibiting:** the child may be impulsive and unable to inhibit inappropriate language or behaviour. This can sometimes result in argumentative or aggressive

responses to certain situations: he cannot easily stop and think about any implications of his actions or words before saying or doing them. He may make comments that are very hurtful. He can be overly affectionate with peers or staff, being unable to control the urge to make physical contact and unaware of the rules of social convention. There can be difficulties inhibiting attention to competing stimuli (e.g. in a busy classroom a child's attention may be directed to activity or noise that is unrelated to the task in hand).

- **Problem solving** and making judgements: these are complex aspects of cognitive activity that are required when obstacles get in the way of achieving a goal. If a strategy does not work the child with ABI may be completely unable to move forward and think of a different way to complete a task. Ylvisaker (1998) describes the steps involved in organised deliberate problem solving as:
  1. identifying the goal and clarifying the problem
  2. gathering and considering information that may be relevant to solving the problem
  3. exploring possible solutions, weighing their relative merits, and choosing the best
  4. formulating a plan of action
  5. executing the plan
  6. monitoring and evaluating the plan's effectiveness.

  Some problems have one correct solution but, as highlighted by Ylvisaker, most real-life problem solving is open-ended in that 'no rule or set of rules determines exactly what information is relevant in thinking about the problem or which of the possible solutions is best.'
- **Self-monitoring:** this relates to difficulties with being able to gauge and evaluate the appropriateness of one's own behaviour. Children with ABI may be oblivious to the reasons for getting into trouble at school and are unable to reflect on the implications of a course of action. They are often unable to benefit from feedback and so may continue to make the same mistakes. A lack of awareness of their deficits makes it hard to make adjustments.
- **Generalising newly acquired skills** to different settings: people with ABI can be very concrete in their thinking, which makes it hard for them to take information about what they have learned and apply it in other situations.
- **Flexibility of thinking:** difficulties may make it hard to cope with change (e.g. a sudden cancellation of an anticipated activity, a deviation from routine procedures, or an unfamiliar member of staff taking charge). Being able to adapt to new and variable situations is an integral part of problem solving.
- **Perseveration:** children with ABI may 'get stuck' on a topic, idea, word or behaviour and repeat it, sometimes incessantly, oblivious to changes in the situation or conversation which make their actions or comments inappropriate.

Normal development and maturation of frontal brain regions emerges in infancy and continues throughout childhood into early adulthood. Development of executive function skills is closely aligned with this and skills develop rapidly throughout childhood. Some executive processes 'come on-line' at an earlier age than others. Key abilities subsumed by the frontal lobes are not, therefore, fully developed until late teens or early adult life. If damage to this area of the brain has affected the normal development of these skills, as is frequently the case following an ABI, this may not be fully apparent in a young child and difficulties only gradually emerge years later.

It is important to remember that many of the difficulties identified above are normal at certain stages of childhood – e.g. inflexible thinking, lack of impulse control, verbal or physical aggressive outbursts and intolerance for delayed gratification are not unusual for a two-year-old, but would be for a twelve-year-old. This highlights the importance of making assessments in the context of a developmental framework.

The greatest difficulties are often not encountered until a child with ABI transfers from primary school. At secondary school children are expected be more independent, to take much greater responsibility for organising the equipment needed for each lesson, to quickly change from one set of tasks to another, or from one room to another in a different part of the school, etc. What may be considered routine tasks, and effortlessly done by most children, can be overwhelming to a child with executive functioning problems.

Executive functioning deficits commonly manifest themselves in behaviour and social difficulties, which are described in more detail in Chapters 7 and 8. The Executive System is an extremely complex one, and further useful information on its development during childhood has been detailed by Anderson (2002).

CHAPTER 5

Planning school integration or reintegration

Successful re-entry requires a great deal of planning, which should begin once the school receives notice that a child has sustained a brain injury.

(Semrud-Clikeman 2001)

It is important to appreciate that rehabilitation following acquired brain injury in childhood is not only a brief service delivered in a medical setting, but a long-term, ongoing effort to help children and their families to achieve realistic goals in the child's everyday environments (Ylvisaker 1998).

Rehabilitation refers to the process of restoring abilities that someone used to have but has lost due to illness or injury. This is in contrast to 'habilitation', which refers to assisting someone to acquire skills they have never had. For children it needs to be a combination of both. Although much reference is made to 'recovery', caution needs to be attached to its use; recovery suggests a return to the level of functioning and skills achieved prior to injury, which, in the case of brain injury, is rarely achievable. Also, as childhood is a process of continuing development, a return to previous or younger levels of functioning is not appropriate.

'Once a child returns to school following acquired brain injury, the educational system becomes the primary service provider for that child' (Ylvisaker *et al.* 1991). The opportunities that schools offer for structured learning programmes, close monitoring, regular and frequent support, and long-term planning make them very well placed to provide ongoing rehabilitation.

'School re-entry is usually an eagerly anticipated milestone along the child's recovery continuum. Too often, the dream becomes a nightmare' (Tucker and Colson 1992). Many parents and children, as well as school staff, perceive the return to school as marking the return to normal life. The good physical recovery that most children make, together with the recovery or retention of the surface features of language, can create an assumption that the return to school will be relatively smooth. It may be anticipated that any additional educational needs can be easily met by existing mainstream and special educational provision and practices. However, many children with acquired brain injury find many of the tasks and expectations – the social, organisational and learning processes – that prior to their injury were well within their capabilities, subsequently problematic. The 'nightmare' referred to by Tucker and Colson above alludes to one or more of a range of issues, e.g. finding it hard to keep up with the pace of work; being misunderstood by school staff; having a rapidly diminishing group of friends; or being denied the degree of independence that peers enjoy.

Returning to school can be a very frightening experience for a child who has had a moderate or severe ABI. The child is often different; different from the person they once were, and different from their peers. He may have had little indication or understanding of those differences while away from the more usual school setting, particularly if any physical difficulties have resolved. These children may have lost the comfortable familiarity of friends at school because of their lengthy absence; they may be returning to a different school; they may have some signs of injury which set them apart from everyone else, and sooner or later after returning they may become distressed when they realise that they are not able to do everyday activities that had previously been carried out effortlessly. Re-entering school confronts the child with reality. If failure is experienced he may quickly lose self-confidence, become de-motivated and develop behaviour difficulties.

As considered in detail in the following chapter regarding assessment, the nature and extent of any difficulties will depend on a variety of factors. This demands a highly individual approach to planning for school re-entry based on each child's individual circumstances. However, there are key features common to successful school reintegration that ideally should be considered as part of a core plan, some of which should be put into action at a very early stage of the child's clinical treatment and continue into the educational setting (Savage and Wolcott 1995). These are set out below.

Joint planning for school re-entry

Preparation for successful school entry or re-entry involves careful planning and organisation well before full-time education is re-established. However, many children currently re-enter school following an ABI without this benefit. Planning requires collaboration between all those involved in the child's health and educational welfare. In addition to family, school staff and relevant medical personnel, it may be useful to include advice from other professionals, such as the educational psychologist; an educational administrator, if resources over and above those that school can provide are required; specialist educational advisers, e.g. for visual impairment, behaviour or learning difficulties; clinical psychologist; and paediatric therapists – each of whom brings a unique perspective and area of expertise. The relationship between them all and quality of communication exchange will greatly influence the process and help to determine the ease with which the child reintegrates to school. Collaboration suggests a need for someone to co-ordinate and disseminate information overall, and so one person must be identified to fulfil this role.

Ideally, initial contact between relevant personnel should take place as soon after the injury as possible. A plan for efficient and effective two-way flow of information needs to be established, as well as identification of the co-ordinator. If the child is admitted to hospital with serious illness or injury it is important for:

- the school to be informed as soon as possible
- a member of school staff to take responsibility for liaison with family and health personnel
- contact and visits to the child to be encouraged when appropriate
- LEA special educational needs administrative section and educational psychology service to be notified. Although it may be unclear in the early stages after injury as to whether any advice or additional provision needs to be made, it can be helpful if the relevant services are informed about special circumstances as soon as possible
- discussions between relevant health and education representatives to be initiated.

Working in partnership with parents

The Special Educational Needs Code of Practice emphasises the key role of the partnership between parents and professionals. Parents have 'unique strengths, knowledge, and experience to contribute to the shared view of a child's needs and the best ways of supporting them' (DfES 2001b: para. 2.2). Key principles that should guide professionals in communicating and working with parents are identified in the Code.

Parents know their child better than anyone else and may be the only ones who are aware of the extent of the changes that the brain injury has caused. However, making plans and decisions about any special educational arrangements can be a complicated and confusing process with which they may have had no previous experience. They may be asked to become involved in this process at the very time that they are already overwhelmed, still struggling to understand what has happened to their child, and juggling a host of other family and work commitments. The notion of parents being equal partners in planning and decision making can sometimes be viewed sceptically by them. It is vital that members of health and education staff consider the emotional, financial and time pressures that parents may be under.

Educational planning can be a difficult and distressing issue for parents. Most parents envisage return to school as part of the continuing process of recovery towards pre-injury levels of academic achievement and social interaction. Their expectation is that life will eventually be as it was before the injury, which is often reinforced by the remarkable recovery of physical skills. It can be a lengthy and difficult process for them to understand and to accept that their child may require some special educational provision (DePompei and Blosser 1994). They may also have to embark on a steep learning curve about special education and participate in what to them is a confusing and complicated process with which they have had no prior experience. There needs to be equal measures of both sensitive support and understanding from staff working with them. In a very small number of cases, parents may be 'disengaged' from the process altogether and it may be up to professionals from each of the statutory agencies to make preparations without their support.

Comprehensive assessment and identification of needs

Comprehensive multi-disciplinary assessment is an essential requirement for effective educational planning and this needs to include information from the child's everyday settings as well as from standardised assessment. Identifying a child's current strengths and needs will help to enable decisions about provision to be made prior to return. More detailed information about assessment is covered in Chapter 6.

Appropriate provision to meet needs

Provision refers to the ways in which needs are met and where they are met. The usual expectation is that children will return to the school that they were attending – or to the educational placement that was planned – prior to injury. However, for various reasons this may no longer be a viable option, e.g. the child's age, or requirements for specialist facilities. Many factors may need to be considered to identify the most appropriate educational setting, such as:

- physical access to buildings
- ongoing medical rehabilitation and provision of therapy
- access to technological equipment
- need for high level of structure
- staff expertise in a range of special educational needs, e.g. communication or sensory difficulties
- social, emotional and behavioural support.

'It would be highly desirable if one could end the dichotomy of 'mainstream' and 'special' schools which together provide a continuum of needs, with the local school as the first to be explored' (Connor 1997).

For the great majority of children with special educational needs there is never any reason to consider provision other than at the local mainstream school. However, if their needs are beyond the resources normally provided in the local school a Statement of

Special Educational Needs may be required, but most children with Statements are educated in mainstream schools. For children with complex needs, it may be necessary to look at a wider range of options, including specialist provision.

Matching a child's needs to what a school can offer is often a case of negotiation, but there is no getting away from the fact that parents, understandably, want what they see as the best provision, while one of the LEA's priority is ensuring the most efficient use of resources. It is important that decisions about appropriate placement are primarily based on the needs of individual children and their family situations.

In-service training of school staff

As educators and parents in the UK are often unaware of the effects that ABI can have on a child's functioning, particularly in relation to cognitive skills and the impact on learning, behaviour and communication, they can be ill-prepared to address the needs of such children and to deal with the difficulties that are frequently faced. There may be little, if anything, in initial or in-service training of teachers and educational psychologists to alert them to the issues related to acquired brain injury that profoundly impact on children's ability to learn and to behave appropriately; issues that can be unique to this population. This lack of awareness is compounded by other professionals who, similarly, have not been made aware of long-term problems that children can experience after acquired brain injury, and most especially when members of the medical profession declare that a good recovery – i.e. physical recovery – has been made.

It is therefore important that educators understand these needs to enable them to plan and provide an appropriate educational programme. Information should be provided which includes:

- What happens in a brain injury
- Details of the particular child's injury
- Recovery patterns
- Immediate and long-term effects of brain injury
- Unique characteristics of acquired brain injury
- Educational interventions that may be useful to consider.

The specific information about the child's injury should include the unique profile of needs, together with details of current strategies that are considered successful.

Helping child, family and peers prepare for return to school

Any absence from school can disrupt peer relationships. School staff must take a lead in keeping the relationships alive. If the child is away from school for a significant time, contact by letter, card, fax, e-mail, phone or video as well as visits can help to sustain friendships and play an important part in maintaining a child's morale.

Alistair received a severe brain injury in a road traffic accident and was in hospital for many months. At his primary school, there was reference to him every day in prayers at assembly and he was sent a weekly letter with contributions from different children. A video of his class was also prepared for him. His class teacher visited him regularly and brought one or two children from the class at each visit. The view of school staff was that they would continue to keep the memory of him alive until he returned.

A critical component of planning for school return is the child's involvement, which needs to be appropriate to his age and level of understanding. He should play as active a role as possible. He may benefit from help to become his own advocate, to be able to communicate his needs.

It is important to ensure that other children at school have factual information about the circumstances surrounding any injury. Inaccurate information can be very damaging and upsetting and information can become easily distorted, like Chinese whispers. In the case of a traumatic brain injury, other children at school may have witnessed the accident.

The informed involvement of other children increases the likelihood of a successful return. How this is dealt with must, if appropriate, first be discussed and agreed with the child who is preparing to return and/or his parents. There must be respect for privacy and preferences when dealing with personal and sensitive details. However, some basic and simple information about the illness or injury can help peers and the child's siblings to make adjustments and accommodate possible changes in relationships. They often remark that their friend has changed, and even the most dedicated friends may eventually lose interest. It can be hard for them to understand how and why changes have occurred and they also need opportunity to express their feelings. Even if the kind of relationship prior to injury is not possible to maintain or re-establish, the quality, warmth and sincerity can still be the same. However, it may require adult intervention and creative thinking to revitalise relationships.

Mohammed had been a popular and confident Year 10 student. He suffered complications after the surgical removal of a brain tumour. He developed hydrocephalus and required the insertion of a shunt. He was also left with some mild cognitive and physical difficulties. He was anxious about how he looked and even more worried about how his peers at school would respond to him. He returned to school, initially on a part-time basis, and he prepared a short talk, which he wanted to present to his tutor group. He included information about what had happened to him, why he now had some physical problems, the shunt that had been inserted, and what his rehabilitation programme consisted of. His form tutor was present and encouraged other students to ask Mohammed questions. Everyone was very pleased with how the session had gone and how useful it had been. Mohammed felt more confident about being back at school after having the topic brought out into the open. Other students showed a high degree of tolerance after being given the opportunity to talk and understand more about what had happened to Mohammed.

The injured child, too, may need much help to understand what has happened to him. This is a complex issue and many people who suffer an acquired brain injury have long-term significant difficulties with this understanding. A reduced level of self-awareness can be frustrating to family and friends, who comment that:

> 'He doesn't think anything has changed.'
> 'He refuses to accept that he cannot do the kind of things he used to do.'

Limited self-awareness can also place the child at increased risk of further injury. Increasing awareness is often a complex issue, and one that has long been recognised as problematic following ABI. It is first of all important to increase the child's knowledge of the events that have happened to him. The cognitive difficulties that may have resulted from the injury make it especially hard for the child to understand, so the task of 'filling in the gaps' and rectifying any misunderstandings or inaccurate knowledge must be delivered in a sensitive way. Compiling an 'autobiography', or life story, starting from the child's very early life, that is age appropriate in its content and presentation, can be very helpful. It also helps to put the illness or injury in a chronological context, which, in years to come, may be helpful for the child with memory difficulties. This could be a gradually evolving project, carried out on a regular and frequent basis using much pictorial information. Presentation in a ring binder allows the child to share any of his contributions to his story, while ensuring that other parts remain private, in what can be a very personal account. Some parents initially find it difficult to go over the events with their child because of their own emotional involvement, but have found it easier to then talk about them in the context of this life story. Indeed they have sometimes benefited themselves from this compilation of events that their child has put together with help, perhaps, from a counsellor or a personal tutor.

The type of information regarding the injury that is included will obviously be related to the child's unique circumstances and family history, as well as his developmental age, but the following list may serve as a useful guide when helping a child to understand the facts and sequences (developed from Beardmore *et al.* 1999):

Story of the accident or illness

- Orientation – when the injury or illness occurred – how long ago?

- Story of the accident or illness – where was it? what happened?

Hospitalisation

- Name of hospital/s
- Length of time in hospital
- Knowledge of hospital procedures or operations.

Brain injury

- Understanding of the term
- Knowledge of brain functioning – appropriate to age or developmental stage
- Knowledge of what happened to the brain when it was injured.

Coma

- Correct description of coma
- Duration of coma.

Long-term effects of brain injury

- Common problems occurring afterwards
- Knowledge of personal deficits, difficulties or disabilities.

Time at home or in rehabilitation before return to school

- Progress and activities.

Additional resources may also be found in life story books, e.g. *My Life and Me* (Camis 2001).

Review and follow-up

The need for ongoing communication between health, education and family personnel after a child has been discharged from the hospital or rehabilitation facility cannot be overstated. After returning home, families can feel isolated and scared. There may be no one in their home area who understands their anxieties and, rather than ameliorating with time, they often increase. The return home can also be the very time when the expertise of the medical staff is most required, ensuring that an effective handover to local or community counterparts has been undertaken, medical advice has been acknowledged and understood, and that liaison with educational staff continues.

Special consideration of preschool children

The impact of an acquired brain injury to a very young child can be devastating. Immature brains are very vulnerable to injury at a crucial time during their development. The younger the child, the fewer the skills that have already been learnt and established. Generally, new learning is more problematic after an ABI than retrieval of previously learnt skills, and therefore young children are at much greater risk for delayed or maladaptive learning than older children because of their more limited knowledge base. There needs to be heightened awareness of the possibility of 'growing into' disability for children who have not yet reached an age at which particular skills are expected to emerge.

A child who is below statutory school age may or may not be attending an early years setting. However, whatever the arrangements for preschool provision, it is important that the local education authority is made aware of any special needs that have resulted from a child's ABI, and that there is provision during the early years as well as careful planning and preparation for the time when the child enters school.

Entering school for the first time with an injured brain can create additional stress factors. It is crucial that members of school staff pay very close attention to the child's learning and behavioural responses and have an awareness of the possible consequences of injury. It is also important to acknowledge the enormous variation of skills and behaviours that can normally be demonstrated by very young children, and to be cautious about over-interpreting. However, early intervention is critical for minimising the negative effects of acquired injury.

Summary

Key points for discussion and action to help ensure successful re-entry to school prior to return should include:

- Identification of child's current strengths and needs
- Staff training about child's brain injury issues
- Return or start date at school
- Plans for phased re-entry. Determine extent of any part-time attendance
- Length of school day
- Plans for social integration and peer support
- Identification of key staff member or personal tutor for liaison and monitoring of child's progress
- Arrangements for rest periods
- Selection of curricular activities best suited to the child's needs and interests and expectations of participation
- Child's timetable and any additional resources or facilities
- Management of unstructured time

- Access to different areas of school (e.g. can stairs be negotiated?)
- Homework policy
- Communication and reporting systems between home and school
- Communication and reporting systems between education and health personnel
- Transport or travel arrangements
- Date of first review.

CHAPTER 6

Issues in the cognitive assessment of children with ABI

The issues associated with cognitive disability after TBI can be exceedingly complex, justifying considerable effort on the part of those charged with helping children with TBI in their pursuit of cognitive improvement and success in daily tasks. Knowledgeable intervention requires a thorough understanding of cognition, its development, its disruption after TBI, and its potential for rehabilitation.

(Ylvisaker and Szekeres 1998)

Assessment is an essential component to enable planning for entering or returning to school after an acquired brain injury. There can be significant cognitive, self-regulatory and sensory deficits resulting from the brain injury and a broad-based assessment is required to identify these.

Many children return to school after an ABI without having a cognitive assessment, and indeed, for children with a mild injury, this may not be required if close monitoring indicates no changes from prior to injury. However, it is important that children who do experience substantial changes in learning or behaviour be referred for a psychological assessment. This chapter is not about how to assess, or which specific tools to consider using, but is to emphasise the significant factors that may need to be taken into account when planning and carrying out assessment of children with ABI.

Psychological assessment

An essential factor in any assessment of a child with ABI is the knowledge and experience of the child psychologist undertaking that assessment. This needs to include:

- **Sound understanding of normal child development**, how and when skills usually emerge and how interruption to development can impact on different cognitive processes at different ages and stages of the development. For example, some behaviours or difficulties commonly associated with ABI and observed or notably absent in a child, particularly a young one, may not be significant or unusual at all in a developmental context.

- **Understanding and experience of paediatric neuropsychology and assessment procedures.** It is now well recognised that many cognitive impairments following acquired brain injury are not detected by clinical neurological examination, nor by commonly used standardised measures of intelligence, and that these are more likely to be identified by neuropsychological assessment (Johnson 1992). A neuropsychological assessment will typically include measures traditionally used by clinical and educational psychologists, as well as additional formal measures that assess a much wider range of cognitive functions. Middleton (2000) emphasises the dangers of using adult models of neuropsychology and assessment tools originally devised for adults. An injury to a developing brain may be qualitatively different to a similar kind of injury in a fully mature adult brain, and so extrapolating information from adult tests or populations and applying it to children may be unsuitable and lack appropriate normative information. Also, tests designed for adults may be of little interest to young children, and do nothing to capture their attention.
- **Familiarity with school systems and sharing of information.** A psychological assessment has very limited value unless it includes information about the implications and recommendations for the child's educational and social environment. It has even less value if that information is not conveyed to the key individuals responsible for the child's learning. The assessment report needs to include an interpretation of test results and other information gathered, using language that can be readily understood by school staff, with practical suggestions and strategies that can be implemented within the context of the school.

Information from the assessment is required in order to help:

- understand changes in learning and behaviour
- identify how the child learns and uses new information
- develop educational goals and an Individual Educational Plan (IEP)
- devise compensatory strategies and evaluate their efficacy
- provide a baseline of cognitive and behavioural strengths and difficulties
- document improvements or changes in functioning
- understand how social, motivational and environmental factors affect performance.

Assessment principles

Multi-disciplinary information

There is no single approach, individual or discipline that can evaluate the spectrum of needs for a child after an acquired brain injury. The factors affecting learning, behaviour and social deficits after an ABI are interrelated, often complex and diverse, and can affect any or many areas of functioning, which cross the boundaries of a number of disciplines and situations. Specific aspects of functioning cannot be assessed and supported in isolation from others. The emphasis must be on the interrelationship between factors involved rather than any of the individual measures or on hypotheses based on areas of the brain which have been damaged.

Information from a variety of settings and from a range of people who bring their different knowledge, perspectives and experience is therefore required in order to understand the full impact of the brain injury, the underlying causes of the child's difficulties, and to formulate recommendations. The uniqueness and diversity of difficulties experienced by each child following ABI precludes a set procedure for assessment.

The overriding issue is the importance of collaboration and a framework which is shared by all involved in any evaluation. Without this there is a danger of over-assessment – different disciplines or professionals using similar tests, or sometimes even the same ones, to assess the same areas of functioning – or under-assessment – some areas of functioning ignored. There can often be considerable overlap of professional areas of interest and it is unacceptable to subject a child to more intrusive assessment procedures than necessary, as well as risking invalidating results due to repetition of the same assessment measures within a short space of time.

It is essential to be aware of the professionals that have been or are currently involved in addition to school staff. These could include any combination of speech and language therapist, occupational therapist, physiotherapist, community paediatrician, neurologist, psychiatrist, social worker, hospital teachers, clinical and/or educational psychologists. This list is by no means exclusive and parents may be best placed to identify who has had contact with their child.

N.B. Clinical assessments of physical, sensory and language skills of children with ABI provide essential information that contributes to an assessment of cognitive functioning. These are outside the scope of this book, but details can be found in Ylvisaker (1998), Appleton and Baldwin (1998), Blosser and DePompei (2003).

Planning for assessment

This should include knowledge of:

- what it is that needs to be assessed
- the sources from which the information is to be obtained
- the assessment approaches and tools.

Assessment may need to be a combination of information about pre-injury functioning in school, social and home environments; perceptions and observations of those who work closely with the child; observation of current functioning in a range of settings; norm referenced and dynamic assessment.

Comparing pre-injury performance and skills with current ones

This helps to identify and explain the extent and nature of the unique cognitive, physical and behavioural changes. A child's functioning prior to injury – skills, achievements, needs, personality, preferences, record of school attendance, etc. – can still have an impact after injury and this is important to know when identifying relevant and realistic goals for change. If a child was experiencing difficulties in a particular area of functioning before injury, it is highly likely that these will continue to be apparent, and may be even more problematic.

Parental contribution

This is a vital part of the process. Parents know their child better than anyone else, and they can provide insights into important aspects of a child's earlier and current functioning that is difficult to glean from anyone else, e.g. relationships with siblings, child's ability to function in the home and in community settings, level and extent of social contacts and activities.

It can be very useful if parents are able to provide information about their child's growth and development, with details of birth, infancy and early childhood, previous medical history, social/emotional development and progress at school. The following checklist may be helpful:

Pre-injury progress

- Developmental milestones and health history
- Progress at school
- Any need for additional help in school (e.g. with reading)
- Any behavioural or emotional difficulties
- Any physical or sensory – sight, hearing, etc. – difficulties
- Out of school interests/hobbies
- Personality (e.g. quiet or extrovert, shy or confident)
- Relationships with family members and friends.

Details of the illness or accident

- The trauma; what happened and when
- The range of functions the injury has affected (e.g. orthopaedic or other injuries)
- Length of stay in hospital
- Any formal rehabilitation – inpatient/outpatient – the child has received and the therapists that were/are involved

Changes and current functioning in:

- Mobility skills (e.g. walking, running, climbing)
- Self-help skills (e.g. eating, drinking, dressing, toileting, etc.). Is any help needed, and if so, how much?
- Sensory skills – vision, hearing, taste, smell, touch
- Conversation – use of words, clarity of speech, speed of talking and responding
- Memory skills (e.g. any difficulties remembering information and any particular strategies that help at home, such as making lists or keeping a diary)
- Attention skills – any specific strategies at home that help with concentration
- Energy levels, rest and sleep (e.g. does the child get more tired now and is this at particular times of the day/week? Any changes to sleep routines)
- Speed of doing tasks (e.g. does it now take any longer to get things done?)
- Behaviour (e.g. any tantrums, anger or aggression, impulsivity, inappropriate behaviour or speech. Any concerns with sexual behaviour)
- Mood and personality (e.g. is the child quieter or more withdrawn?)
- Friendships and social life (e.g. does the child initiate social contact with others of similar age, maintain friendships from prior to the injury or spend much time alone?)
- Leisure time activities – how is time out of school spent (e.g. hobbies, interests, etc). Can he play or organise time constructively when alone?
- Independence (e.g. in what ways is the child now more reliant on others? Are there any safety issues as a result of the injury?)

Parental views about the child's progress at school

- Areas in which the child experiences most success
- Current difficulties
- Ability to concentrate and to finish tasks
- Changes in reading, writing and spelling skills
- Changes in the child's ability to remember, organise, plan, problem solve and reason
- Successful approaches that help the child learn (e.g. extra help or strategies)
- The child's ability to manage changing classes or teachers, and unexpected changes to the routine
- Any difficulties at break or lunchtimes
- If homework is expected, are there any particular issues with it (e.g. can the child organise and complete it independently)? Is much assistance required and given?

- Does he like school and want to go?
- Is he reasonably organised – for a child of that age – with school books and equipment, clothes, jobs at home, etc.?
- To what extent is the child aware of any learning, behaviour or social changes?

Parental views about the child's needs in school

- What are the child's special educational needs considered to be?
- Are they being well met? If not, what is required?
- Do they have any concerns regarding the child's present and future education?
- What are the most important rehabilitation/educational goals?

Effects on the whole family

- Effects that the child's illness or injury has had on the family as a whole and the relationships within it.

Child's contribution to assessment

As well as being the subject of the assessment process, it is also essential that, if at all possible, the child be enabled to make any views known and be a legitimate partner in decision making resulting from assessment. This can sometimes be a particularly challenging issue given the cognitive and communication deficits that may be experienced. Age, too, is a determining factor. However, a lack of awareness of deficits or difficulties in communication should in no way preclude involvement and there are many ways in which decisions can be made with a child rather than for a child. DfES (2001c) provides advice for ways in which young people can be encouraged to participate in assessment and decision making.

Blosser and DePompei (2003) provide pertinent questions – adapted below – that can be asked of young people who have returned to school after an injury. These can be used and adapted in a discussion or written format, depending on a child's capabilities:

1. What problems are you experiencing in class? What are the problems that you are having since you returned to school?
2. How do you usually act when you are experiencing problems or frustrations in class? List some of the ways you behave when you are having problems.
3. What classroom situation causes you the most problems?
   a) Noise
   b) Temperature
   c) Pictures and wall decorations
   d) Other people in the room
   e) Other things

4. What are the ways people – your teachers/assistants/classmates – help you when you experience trouble in class?
5. What do you think people should do to help you?
6. What things do people do to frustrate you or cause you more problems?
7. What do you think people should **stop** doing when they are around you?
8. At what time of day do you do your best?
   a) Early morning
   b) Mid-morning
   c) Around the middle of the day
   d) Mid-afternoon
   e) Early evening
   f) Late evening

   Why do you think this is your best time of day?
9. If you could choose three skills to improve, what would they be?
10. What are five things that are great about you that you would like other people to know?

Functions to be assessed

General intellectual ability

- Verbal
- Non-verbal

Attention/concentration

- Visual
- Auditory

Language and communication

- Expressive language
- Receptive language
- Written language

Memory and learning

- Visual/Auditory
- Immediate/Delayed
- Recall/Recognition

Perception

- Visual

- Visual/Motor
- Auditory
- Sensory

Speed of information processing

- Motor speed
- Thinking speed

Executive skills

- Planning and organising
- Initiating
- Goal setting
- Inhibiting
- Problem solving
- Self-monitoring
- Flexibility of thought

Orientation

- Time
- Place
- Person

Educational attainments

- Reading – accuracy, comprehension, fluency, speed
- Spelling
- Recording – handwriting, word-processing
- Maths – arithmetic, reasoning

Personality: adjustment and behaviour at school and home

- Social skills
- Self-concept
- Behavioural control
- Frustration tolerance

Additional considerations that may impact on assessment of cognitive functioning

Stamina and fatigue	School attendance
Consistency of performance	Insight/awareness
Health/medical conditions	Effects of medication
Interests and preferences	Attitudes and fears
Cultural factors	First/foreign language factors

Limitations of standardised assessment

Standardised measures can be very useful for assessing a wide range of skills that may be affected by ABI. They also enable comparison of a child's performance with that of others of the same age and provide a measure of change over time, indicating if there has been deterioration or gains in performance.

An understanding of the unique issues of ABI in children includes an appreciation that test scores can overestimate a child's functioning in the classroom and other real-life situations. Most assessments provide estimates of a child's optimal rather than typical levels of functioning. Results may be misleading and there is a danger of false optimism if the following are not taken into account:

- Scores may reflect a good recovery of skills learnt prior to the ABI rather than current learning abilities.
- Attention deficits in a busy classroom may not be obvious in a quiet assessment setting that offers one-to-one interaction.
- Decreased endurance or persistence may not be apparent if the presented tasks are short and novel.
- Impaired initiation, planning and organisation skills may not be observable in a highly structured setting with provision of precise, unambiguous instructions and when the criteria for success are clearly specified.
- Memory and information-processing demands during the duration of an assessment session may not be the same as those involved in the carry over of information from lesson to lesson or week to week, as is expected in a typical school setting.
- A one-off assessment session does not make allowances for frequent inconsistencies in performance that can be experienced in children with ABI.
- Continued change and recovery of lost or impaired skills can restrict the usefulness of test results.

(Adapted from Ylvisaker *et al.* 1994)

Intelligence testing

Traditional IQ tests 'tap' what has already been learnt and therefore do not usually reflect significant deficits after brain injury. Even children who have had a moderate to severe injury, which results in significant learning difficulties, may score within the normal range on a standardised intelligence test. Measurements of verbal IQ can sometimes provide an estimate of pre-injury status because skills acquired prior to injury are often preserved or recover relatively quickly. The performance IQ gives a better measure of loss and improvement because visuo-perceptual and visuo-motor skills are not so easily recovered, and the ability to learn new skills, solve problems and work at speed is most commonly affected.

Dynamic assessment

This offers an approach that is an alternative, or a supplement, to normative testing measures and the principles lend themselves very well to working with children with ABI (Ylvisaker and Gioia 1998). Dynamic assessment focuses on a child's ability to learn, and not on what has already been learnt. In conventional testing situations, the examiner presents items to a child and records the response without any attempt to intervene in order to guide, or improve, the child's performance. Information from traditional 'static' tests are a snapshot and do not necessarily provide any indication of a child's potential for change. Dynamic assessment aims to evaluate the ability of the child to learn from interaction with a teacher, through observation of the child's responsiveness to instruction and guidance on particular tasks. The strategies used in dynamic assessment are more closely related to the kind of learning processes that already take place in schools and other real-life environments – e.g. the teacher asks leading questions, demonstrates, starts to solve a task and asks the child to continue. The ability to learn is based on the premise that a child's knowledge develops during interactions with more capable others. Acquisition of new learning initially requires maximum assistance from an adult but gradually the child develops greater responsibility for the activity/learning task as the information becomes internalised. The aim of the assessment process is to evaluate the amount of change that can occur during the interactions with the examiner, the focus being not so much on *what* a child learns but more on *how much* and *what kinds of information and guidance* are required in order for learning to occur. Dynamic assessment has been reported to provide 'down to earth and usable advice for teachers and special needs assistants as a direct result of assessment' (Deutsch and Reynolds 2000). There is considerable interest in the use of this assessment approach, and it is becoming more widely practised by psychologists, endorsed by government support for the teaching of thinking skills. Further information about dynamic assessment can be found in Birnbaum and Deutsch (1996), Tzuriel (2001), Sternberg and Grigorenko (2002).

Functional assessment

There may well be significant benefit in carrying out some individual assessment tasks, which require the assessor and child to work away from the classroom in a distraction-free area, but much information that is useful needs to be gathered from functional settings and from those who work in them with the child. This kind of information would typically be obtained using a range of methods from observation, interviews with school staff, questionnaires or inventories, records of the child's school work, National

Curriculum information, etc. Obviously the younger the child, the more limited the availability of educational information. Contact with a preschool child's community service providers, e.g. Health Visitor, playgroup/nursery staff, may therefore be helpful.

Assessment of contextual/environmental factors

Although the focus of an assessment is the child, he does not exist in isolation and must be considered in relation to his environment. The importance of ongoing contextualised assessment cannot be overstated. Factors in home, school or community life in which the child may be experiencing difficulties must be taken into account. Children interact with school staff, family, friends, peers, etc., all of whom will influence a child's learning and social behaviours, to a lesser or greater extent.

It is also important to remember that, as indicated above, a child's abilities in the kind of atypical setting that usually occurs when standardised normative assessment is carried out – e.g. a one-to-one, relatively distraction free, highly structured situation – can lead to overestimates of actual abilities in the classroom. Within a busy classroom, during a normal school day, a child's ability to attend, plan, organise and problem solve will be taxed to a much greater extent. What is just as important as assessing the skills or knowledge that children possess is how or whether they are able to use that knowledge. Children with ABI may have theoretical knowledge but be unable to apply that to functional situations.

Many factors within the school setting may have considerable impact on a child's ability to learn and to behave appropriately and, therefore, need to be considered when assessing and making recommendations.

Environmental factors

Ethos of school and management style
Class size
Acknowledgement of needs
Behaviour policy
Current ways of supporting any difficulties
Consistency of staff
Cues or prompts
Activity level
Routines
Noise
Lighting
Temperature

Length of concentrated learning periods
Seating position and arrangements
Peer models
Classroom space
Peer support
Reinforcement frequency
Degree of structure
Availability of choice
Classroom organisation
Playground management
Management of dining arrangements
Transitions – transferring from class to class

Instructional factors

Task level and clarity
Task adaptations/differentiation
Expectations/differentiation
Time restrictions
Opportunities for success
Equipment
Task performance
Auditory demands
Task familiarity
Attentional demands
Visual demands
Memory demands
Task interest
Task length
Homework demands
Verbal reinforcement
Pace of delivering
Recapping of previous learning
Opportunities for rehearsal/practice
Changes in activity
Reading demands
Frequency of feedback
Teaching style and mode of instruction
Teacher and other adult support
Advance organisers
Task format

Reporting assessment information

A written report is usually the most lasting part of an assessment and can be the most effective way of recording and conveying information gathered during the process. However, there needs to be awareness that it can also be the least efficient way of communicating information if the report fails to be seen by those in a position to implement recommendations. Reports can easily be filed away without the advice in them being brought to the notice of school staff who work directly with the child. It is important that the person who conducted the assessment makes direct contact with the parents and the school's Special Educational Needs Co-ordinator (SENCO) or other relevant members of staff to discuss the implications of the written report. This ensures that the most pertinent information reaches them, and also the personal contact can encourage the school staff to take greater interest in the issues and responsibility for the implementation of the recommendations.

Assessment after an acquired brain injury very often focuses on loss, particularly on the areas of functioning with which the child currently has difficulties. It is important to acknowledge positive aspects by including information about a child's strengths, abilities and interests.

Feedback to the child who has been assessed is also important. This can usually be done verbally, using clear, simple language that is meaningful for the child, explaining strengths and needs honestly with examples and analogies. It is vital that the child is not overwhelmed and is helped to see any problems that are described as manageable. The pupil needs to be an integral part of any process of change and therefore negotiation and agreement of simple structured objectives will increase the likelihood for success of any plans to be put into effect.

Periodic and ongoing evaluation

Assessment of a child following ABI must be viewed as an ongoing procedure. An initial cognitive assessment may have been carried out while a child was attending a hospital or rehabilitation centre as either an in-patient or out-patient. This information is useful for helping to determine the needs and kinds of support to be put into place when the child returns to school. However, there will be additional and important information as the child adapts to the environment and, after a period of settling in and orientating to the longer-term setting, it is essential to assess how cognitive impairments impact on a child's ability to successfully integrate socially and academically, i.e. how the child is learning and behaving over time in a more usual environment. It is also easier for the child to be actively involved in the process of assessment and review when back in a familiar environment.

Because of the nature of recovery after ABI, assessments need to be undertaken more often than is normally the case with other children. Children with ABI have a more frequently changing profile of skills and needs than their peers and some information can quickly become outdated. They may demonstrate rapid improvements in some skill areas and make very limited gains in others. Some problems may not be evident until years after injury, making ongoing monitoring essential in order to appreciate the extent of any resulting developmental difficulties.

Commonly, there is a cumulative effect of the damage on the rate of development and so there is often a widening of the gap in relation to peers over time. This means that the learning challenges increase for children with ABI as they progress through the key stages. Informal monitoring and appraisal should be ongoing at school and this is an important source of information for determining the appropriate level of tasks and support. National Curriculum information contributes to this too and helps to make comparisons with other children at the same key stage, which parents in particular find useful for gauging how their child is progressing. A very frequent parental question is: How is my child doing compared to everyone else in the class? Reassessment using psychometric measures – a way of assessing a person's skills, or ability, or aspects of personality in a structured, standardised way that enables comparison with others – may also be useful to ascertain changes in a child's skills over time.

CHAPTER 7

Understanding and managing behaviour changes

> *The loss of behavioral control is a reaction to an impaired brain attempting unsuccessfully to understand a complex environment. It is an attempt to simplify or alter the environment to the level that the head injured child or adolescent is able to manage appropriately and minimize behavioral expressions of confusion, frustration, or failure. Rarely can these procedures be identified or implemented by the head injured child or adolescent directly. Instead these techniques depend on other people to evaluate what specifically is overwhelming the head injured child, monitoring the environment for the head injured child, and implementing procedures to reduce the environmental complexity.*
>
> (Lehr 1990)

Changes in personality and behaviour are common following ABI. Of all the difficulties, that may occur families rate behaviour change as the most persistent, disruptive and disturbing of problems. Behavioural challenges are often, over and above any other presenting problem, the most difficult to tolerate in schools and the most significant barrier to integration. How a child behaves, rather than how much a child learns, can frequently be what determines the suitability or success of a school placement. Changes in behaviour following ABI do not often resolve quickly or spontaneously. Also, generally, the longer the child experiences them the harder they are to remediate and the more severe they can become.

Teachers often fail to associate behaviour difficulties with an ABI, especially if there has been any time lapse between the injury and the presenting behaviours. As described in Chapter 3, there may be delayed deficits resulting from injury, and behaviour difficulties may not emerge until months or even years after the trauma.

An understanding of a child's brain injury and the impact that this can have on cognitive, communicative and psychosocial functioning enables school staff to be aware of potential difficulties and therefore make provision to avoid or to minimise them.

Behaviour at acute stage of recovery

Stages of cognitive improvements and related behaviours immediately after an ABI resulting in coma have been well documented and descriptions of these stages, or levels of disability, have been organised into scales, e.g. The Rancho Scale (Malkmus and Stenderup 1974), the Disability Rating Scale (Rappaport *et al.* 1982). References to these may be helpful during early stages of recovery to help explain the long-term processes of improvement from serious brain injuries. In the acute stages after injury children are often confused and agitated, as described in Chapter 2. Beyond the acute stages of recovery, more persistent, longer-term behaviour changes may emerge due to deficits in complex cognitive and psychosocial areas of functioning. It is these enduring, and sometimes later emerging problems that create barriers to academic and social success.

Longer-term behaviour difficulties

Behaviour changes can range from subtle difficulties to those that are considered to be very disruptive and challenging. Many of the behaviours experienced by children with ABI are also exhibited by non-injured children, but the frequency and intensity is often much greater in the child with ABI.

Common behavioural difficulties following ABI can include:

Impulsivity
Disinhibition
Poor motivation
Anger outbursts
Dependency
Stubbornness
Denial
Apathy
Immaturity
Inflexibility
Irritability
Aggression
Sexual inappropriateness
Egocentricity
Emotional lability
Lethargy

Some of the above issues relate to excesses of behaviour, but it is also important to appreciate that there can be a reduction of behavioural responses as a result of brain injury, which can also be challenging to educators. Damage to brain mechanisms responsible for arousal and initiation can be manifested as apathy or lethargy and children may be described as lazy or lacking in motivation. There is often an assumption that the ability to attend and to initiate tasks is automatic and therefore any failure to do so is a wilful decision on the part of a child. Also, apathy or lethargy are not generally deemed to be as problematic for school staff as the managing of disruptive behaviours, because there is not such a negative impact on other individuals, nor does it necessarily divert a teacher's attention to the extent of being unable to deliver a planned lesson. There may, therefore, be less attempt to address the needs of children who are passive.

It is important to appreciate that significant limitations in behavioural responses can be just as worrying because they can interfere with successful learning and socialising as much as any excesses of behaviour.

After ABI there may be few if any behaviour changes or there may be many. Some children may grow out of certain behaviours and go on to develop more appropriate ways of responding, or else the behaviours may be replaced by equally inappropriate but different ones. The intensity and frequency will also vary depending on a number of factors. There can be different reasons why they occur and an understanding of these can help to manage them effectively. Invariably most behaviours are a complex mix of factors and the result of interaction between the child and the school, the family, and the wider community. However, ABI often creates additional issues that contribute to behaviour changes and difficulties.

Reasons for behaviour change after brain injury

Neurological damage to the brain

This can result in direct behavioural consequences. The parts of the brain responsible for self-regulatory mechanisms are commonly injured, resulting in reduction of a child's ability to control his own behaviour. Disinhibition, impulsivity, reduced anger control, and aggressiveness are often observed in children with ABI. These consequences may be delayed and may emerge when executive functioning skills fail to mature.

Pre-injury behaviour problems

Behaviour difficulties after an ABI can be a reflection and/or magnification of problems experienced before the injury. There is much research to demonstrate that personality styles, behaviour patterns and family dynamics influence behavioural outcome. There is an over-representation of children with traumatic brain injury who had social adjustment difficulties prior to injury. Although brain injury increases the risk of behaviour difficulties, it is important to appreciate that behaviour difficulties increase the risk of brain injury! It is therefore essential to consider pre-injury behavioural functioning before attributing any behavioural disturbance to the injury.

Psychological reactions associated with disability

Many behaviour changes observed after an ABI are not a direct consequence of the injury but of the circumstances following it, particularly the child's reaction to this and to the changes that have occurred as a result of it. Of most significance is the ability to deal with significant loss and change, e.g. loss of friends and social status; loss of independence; loss of previous academic and cognitive abilities or levels of success; and loss of physical function. These can all have a profound impact on a child's emotional state and self-image. The child may no longer have the ability to function in the way he did before and therefore not have control over situations as he previously had. Feelings of failure and frustration can lead to acting out or withdrawal. Children may demonstrate strong emotional outbursts as a reaction to what they consider to be unreasonable restrictions on desired activities. Cognitive deficits after ABI, such as impaired judgement, impulsivity or disinhibited behaviour, can lead to a child's greater risk taking. This raises concerns, particularly among parents, about safety issues, but close supervision by adults may be resented. This often becomes an increasingly contentious issue between parents and a child with ABI as the normal expectation for independence increases in adolescence. Safety issues around contact sports, road sense, drugs and sexual behaviour are common sources of friction and any perceived intervention, control or restrictions by a parent can lead to an escalation of a child or adolescent's behavioural outbursts.

Environmental factors

As previously mentioned, there are many studies to indicate that the influence of the home environment is a contributory factor towards behavioural outcome after brain injury. There is a much greater risk of new behavioural problems – i.e. problems that did not exist prior to injury – in children with home environments that include significant psychosocial adversity (Ylvisaker and Feeney 1998). Children with brain injury are more dependent on a positive and supportive family environment than neurologically normal children (Taylor *et al.* 2002). Parents may have limited resources to respond to new problems, or they may already be too burdened by other stressful issues to be able to provide opportunities that encourage behavioural adjustment.

Cognitive and communicative impairment

Behaviour problems can be associated with difficulties children have in understanding what is required of them, or a lack of ability to carry out requested tasks. Situations can demand more skills than a child has the capacity to cope with – e.g. they may be too demanding, confusing or over-stimulating. The range of cognitive deficits that they now experience can result in a high level of frustration, which increases the negative behaviours. Feeney and Ylvisaker (1997) indicate that cognitive, behaviour and communication problems following brain injury are frequently 'alternative descriptions of the same underlying reality' – i.e. what is termed inappropriate behaviour may be due to communication deficits; problems with planning and organising goal-directed behaviour; lack of insight about limitations; forgetfulness; inability to transfer behaviour that has been learned from one context to another; or rigidly sticking to ways of doing tasks that were successful in the past.

Medication

Anti-convulsant or other medication may affect a child's learning capabilities and behaviour. There may also be a number of interrelated factors if changes are noted when children are on medication, all of which will need to be appraised. Any such concerns should be discussed with the child's doctor as well as with other school staff.

Communicative intent of behaviour

'There is typically an important purpose served by behaviour, no matter how unusual or objectionable that behaviour may appear' (Feeney and Ylvisaker 1997). Almost all conscious behaviours are a way of communicating. A child's behaviour is a way of coping with the world and its frustrations. Children with ABI frequently have verbal communication deficits, along with a range of cognitive difficulties, and these are exacerbated by fatigue, anxiety, confusion, disorientation, etc. Whenever any of these negative feelings are experienced it is often not possible for a child to talk fluently enough to express this, or to say what he would like to have changed. Behaviour is often his only language; he does not necessarily choose to misbehave but may not possess any other skills under certain conditions.

When a child is experiencing behaviour difficulties, it is important to consider what message he may be trying to convey. For instance, it may be to express: boredom; that the work is too difficult; a need for attention; a delight in getting a reaction which is entertaining; a feeling of being tired or overwhelmed; a measure of control; frustration because of unpleasant comments from peers. Identifying the communicative intent is a first step towards providing alternative, more positive ways to replace unwanted behaviour.

Managing behaviour in school

Teaching or helping children in the classroom to behave in socially acceptable ways is an integral part of the wider educational process for enabling young people to be as independent as possible.

All schools under the jurisdiction of the Department for Education and Skills (DfES) are required to publish a behaviour and anti-bullying policy. Although some of the behavioural difficulties seen in children with ABI may need to be addressed differently from those of other children, clear expectations for appropriate behaviour should always be maintained. This, therefore, is not at odds with approaches to behaviour management which are planned and agreed at a whole-school level. Parents, children and staff all need to be aware of the clear procedures for managing behaviour. School approaches to behaviour management may involve consequential strategies, as described below.

Use of consequences

Having consequences in place is essential for the successful running of an organisation. Most people learn to behave according to expected consequences, i.e. they do what is likely to result in something that is rewarding, or they avoid doing something that could have an unwanted outcome for them. Behaviour management policies and practices in schools are often based on principles that primarily focus on delayed consequences. In some schools, the identified consequences may be entirely negative, i.e. sanctions that are applied if rules are violated with no emphasis on positive consequences, i.e. outcomes for children who comply with school rules.

Consequential management of behaviour is linked to an assumption that children have intact neurological mechanisms for:

- an understanding of cause and effect
- remembering what they have to do to achieve or to avoid a particular outcome
- understanding that a particular outcome may be delayed, i.e. exercising some degree of self-control
- being able to generalise from one situation to another.

Children with ABI may have suddenly lost these cognitive skills, which are rarely clearly identified because, for most people, they are part of an automatic or effortless repertoire that has been gradually acquired or learnt during developmental progress.

The use of **positive consequences** is very important; all children need to be acknowledged and rewarded for appropriate behaviour, including children with ABI. However, the behaviour of children with ABI needs to be managed and supported primarily by antecedent control (see below).

Children, parents and all school staff need to know what the consequences are for misbehaviour and this must be part of a whole-school policy. It is important to understand, though, that **negative consequences** do not help children with ABI to behave appropriately. Some strategies commonly used in schools may even exacerbate the very behaviours that they aim to eliminate. Reprimands given when a child is already experiencing a high level of stress or excitement can result in an explosive outburst.

Delayed consequences are commonly ineffective for managing behaviour provoked by ABI: they may fail to act either as a 'brake' for inappropriate behaviour or as an incentive to behave in desirable ways because:

- Difficulties with memory, organisation of thoughts and with problem solving may mean that potential consequences cannot be anticipated, i.e. they are often not able to choose a course of action based on what is likely to happen later.
- ABI frequently damages the parts of the brain responsible for monitoring and inhibiting behaviour, so providing few internal resources for control. When a child

with ABI begins to lose control there is an inverse capacity to self-regulate this, i.e. the more he loses control the less able he is to stop what he is doing. When behaviours begin to escalate, more resources are required of the adult in charge. 'It is like the proverbial water going over the dam. Once behaviours begin to escalate it is more difficult for teachers and parents to manage the behaviours' (Savage *et al.* 2001).

- Delayed reprimands often have little meaning for children with ABI, who may have limited recollection about the events for which they are being admonished.
- The use of sanctions, by themselves, does not help children learn more appropriate behaviours.

Murray had been hit by a car when he was nine years old and sustained an ABI. He made a good physical recovery and was very keen to get back to school to rejoin his friends. At age 13, he was attending a mainstream comprehensive school. He was described as below average ability, disorganised and forgetful. He was generally liked by staff, but viewed as immature and silly by peers. He was often teased and called names because of his slowness to respond, especially when a topic of conversation had moved on and his verbal contributions to discussions were considered to be inappropriate or irrelevant. Murray was sensitive to criticism and reacted aggressively, mostly verbally but sometimes physically, which tended to happen when no adult was in earshot to keep name-calling at bay. On one occasion in class Murray had been 'wound up' excessively, resulting in him physically lashing out at another boy. The two of them were sent to see the deputy head teacher, who was busy and so they had to wait until he was free to talk to them. By the time this happened, Murray had very limited recall of the classroom dynamics that had led to the assault, but was asked to describe in detail what had happened, which he was unable to do. The other teenage boy was able to provide an articulate account of himself as a ' victim' of an unprovoked attack, which then engendered further agitation and verbal abuse from Murray. This lent additional credibility to the 'victim's' account and to Murray being perceived as the troublemaker. He was denied privileges and put on report.

Prevention

Preventing problems before they occur, or interrupting behaviours before they escalate, is about managing environments to enable children to control their behaviour and to experience success. **Antecedent control** is a positive, proactive approach, as opposed to reacting to problems, i.e. dealing with them after they have happened. If internal mechanisms for regulating behaviour have been damaged or destroyed, then there is a need for external supports to help children to behave appropriately. Focusing on the antecedents that are most likely to cause an escalation of unwanted behaviours, and managing the environment to prevent them from happening, is much more effective than expecting the child with ABI to remember the rules and to abide by them. Antecedent management of behaviour:

- reduces or eliminates unwanted behaviours
- creates a more calm, positive and productive working environment for everyone
- gives a child greater control of the environment
- allows a child greater accomplishment and success
- provides many other long-term benefits (e.g. raised self-esteem)
- removes the focus on punitive action
- teaches adaptive skills to all children.

Understanding the brain injury and the impact it has had on a child's cognitive functioning helps education staff to use strategies that prevent, or minimise, problematic behaviour from either starting or escalating out of control. The most effective way to do this is to predict when unwanted behaviours are likely to occur. Knowing the triggers enables environmental changes to be made that will minimise the likelihood of that behaviour occurring.

Consistent approach

Behaviour rarely changes overnight and some children may have had years to develop ways of behaving that are inappropriate. Children's behavioural repertoires can also be very limited if they have lost the skills that had served them well prior to injury. There are also no such things as 'quick-fix' behavioural programmes or solutions. School staff may claim they have 'tried everything' but that nothing has worked. It may be the case that several different strategies have been used, but each of them only for a short time, or only when the member of staff has remembered to use them, or only by some of the adults who work with the children. Consistency is crucial to help children with ABI learn to behave appropriately and this can only happen if everyone applies the same rules in the same way. It also encourages greater understanding and support among colleagues. Shared concerns and support are crucial for individual members of staff to feel confident in handling difficult situations in the classroom. If a strategy appears to be unsuccessful, it is important to examine the extent to which consistency is being applied:

- Do all members of staff have the same expectations for behaviour in any given situation, such as in the classroom, the dining hall, the playground, in the corridors, on the school bus, etc.?

- Are expectations clearly defined for pupils and staff, leaving no ambiguity about interpretations of what is appropriate, i.e. what actually must be seen to constitute appropriate behaviour? A child with ABI will benefit from being reminded of the rules and expectations each time a particular situation is about to occur.
- Are there frequent verbal and visual opportunities for everyone to be reminded about the rules of behaviour? Are they prominent in visual form, such as in an eye-catching notice on every classroom wall or other situations specific to the relevant behaviour? Children with ABI may genuinely not know how to behave in certain situations and will often take their cue from other information around them. If the only cue is another child behaving inappropriately they may well follow suit.
- Are rewards applied consistently? It is far more preferable to focus on appropriate behaviour and reward it, than to give more attention to undesirable behaviour. It enhances the positive atmosphere in the class and is usually very reinforcing. Even children who frequently display unwanted behaviours are appropriate some of the time, which makes it all the more important to acknowledge the times they are doing so.
- Are all children rewarded? Children with ABI need encouragement, recognition and reinforcement about acceptable ways of behaving.
- Do children and staff know what the consequences are for breaking rules? These must not be subjectively decided by individual members of staff, but must be part of an agreed whole-school policy, i.e. a planned rather than an impulsive approach.
- Are sanctions applied consistently? Children can quickly get to know the members of staff who threaten sanctions for misdemeanors but who never carry them out or do so inconsistently. This increases the likelihood of continued inappropriate behaviour.
- Is rule breaking handled consistently calmly?

Functional assessment of behaviour

> No matter how bad a child's behaviour seems, it is important to remember that most children are driven to succeed and that at any given time they are probably doing the best they can with the abilities they have.
>
> (Deaton 1994)

Behavioural assessment and behaviour change are not processes that are 'done to' or 'carried out on' a child, nor are they to be confused with crisis management. A behavioural assessment involves understanding what triggers particular behaviour in a context; ascertaining what the communicative intent or function of the child's behaviour is; and identifying the environmental, instructional, affective and other factors that appear to lead to and maintain the behaviour. This information enables changes to be made to enhance the probability of increasing appropriate behaviour and decreasing problematic behaviour. The intensity of any behavioural intervention needs to match the intensity of the child's behaviour. Most assessments and interventions in the classroom are low-key, quick to implement and immediately rectify situations that are considered inappropriate, e.g. the class teacher may see a child becoming quickly over-excited and not attending to task when papers start blowing around the classroom due to a draft. The situation can be easily rectified and the child redirected after closing the window or door. More systematic, structured functional assessment is required when behaviours frequently interfere with the learning or safety of any of the children in class.

Changing aspects of a young person's behaviour needs to be carefully considered within a collaborative problem-solving process; in other words it is important to involve school staff, parents and the child, if it is age-appropriate to do so. This establishes a team approach to acknowledge the situations in which there are unwanted behaviours. Mutual respect and co-operation is vital in managing behavioural problems and acceptance that all concerned have an important role to play. Directly involving the child and family as much as possible can increase their motivation for changing situations and for understanding the reasons for doing so. Knowing how a child behaves at home and strategies that are successful there may provide useful insights when trying to ascertain appropriate interventions at school. Also, parental endorsement of a behavioural programme at school and reinforcement at home can increase consistency and therefore the likelihood of success. To change behaviour it is crucial to carry out an assessment of the behaviour and the factors that contribute to it. A common mistake is to try to implement a strategy before going through the processes set out below:

Specify the behaviour

To change behaviour it is necessary to specify exactly what the child does that needs to change. Words such as 'lazy', 'disruptive', 'rude', 'aggressive', 'hyperactive' may sometimes be considered useful shorthand in general conversation but the terms do not indicate what the behaviour is. Descriptions such as: 'gets out of seat many times during the lesson', 'shouts obscenities when asked to do a writing task', 'swings his arm out and strikes another child that he passes in the corridor' are behaviours that can be observed and measured. Care needs to be taken when choosing words to describe behaviour to make sure that everyone in the team understands and also that they do not apportion blame. There may be a number of unwanted behaviours, but it is important to prioritise and attempt to change just one or two behaviours at a time. Also, focusing on the implementation of a positive behaviour can sometimes reduce a number of other undesirable behaviours if they directly compete with it. For instance, Janine frequently does not carry out the tasks she is asked to do; gets out of her seat many times during the lesson; wanders around the classroom; talks to other children; starts to fiddle with equipment and other materials in the room; and shouts out comments about other children's work that is on display. There are a number of different behaviours there! Identifying one of the behaviours to change, such as getting out of her seat during lesson time, will inevitably have a knock-on effect on the other disruptive behaviours; if she stays in her seat she is not carrying out the other disruptive actions.

Identify the features of the behaviour and those associated with it

Behaviour almost always serves a purpose and takes place in an identifiable context. The contextual setting, what happens before a particular behaviour, and what immediately follows the behaviour are important in order to ascertain what is maintaining this. A-B-C approaches to recording behaviour are so called because they:

A – describe **ANTECEDENTS** to the behaviour, i.e. events which occur prior to it and which may trigger it
B – describe the specific **BEHAVIOUR**
C – describe the **CONSEQUENCES** of the behaviour, i.e. the events which immediately follow it and which may reinforce it.

Other direct observations in the settings in which the unwanted behaviour occurs are important to record as well, as they may help to explain the reasons for this.

Keeping records of what is observed is necessary for successful behaviour change. Accurate information is required prior to implementing a behaviour change strategy in order to establish:

- how long the behaviour continues each time it occurs – its duration
- how many times it occurs – its frequency
- where and when it occurs
- who else is there
- what is going on at the time the behaviour occurs.

Once a system has been agreed and established for daily observations of behaviour, recording does not have to be time consuming or complicated. It may be helpful to draw up a simple chart.

Identify the purpose of the behaviour

It is important to consider the communicative intent of the child and the ways in which the behaviour benefits him, e.g. gaining attention, avoiding a task, or sensory stimulation. Often the function of a behaviour is:

- to avoid or escape from something (e.g. a task, a person or an event)
- to obtain something (e.g. attention, control or a particular activity)
- to express a feeling (e.g. discomfort, excitement, anxiety or surprise).

The purpose of a behaviour is not always immediately evident and so gathering more information about the child and the wider context can help to ascertain what function it serves.

Identify the contributing factors: the wider context

In addition to the specific and immediate contextual events – i.e. the antecedents to the behaviour – assessment information for behaviour change needs to include a wider appreciation of the environmental, instructional and within-child factors, such as those listed in Chapter 6, as examination of these may help to explain the reasons for the behaviour. Some of these may not necessarily be factors that can be changed, e.g. fatigue, but an understanding of them can help to determine the most appropriate ways to support a child with ABI.

To understand the wider context, it may be necessary to gather information from many different sources using a variety of methods, e.g. observation, the child's school records, behaviour checklists, interviews with the child, the parents and other school staff.

Summarise information and make hypotheses

After the information has been gathered, it should be discussed with parents and relevant school staff and a hypothesis drawn up about the child and the behaviour. A hypothesis is a suggested statement about the relationship between the behaviour and other factors.

e.g. When this occurs ... Jennifer does ... in order to ...

The information and hypothesis can help to focus further questions that may enable those involved to understand and address unwanted behaviour.

e.g. Does the child have the skills for meeting the demands of the situation in which the problematic behaviour occurs?

Do the other pupils sitting close by help or hinder the situation?

Does the behaviour only happen at certain times of day and in certain places?

Are there additional health or family factors?

A child's angry outbursts may be triggered by a request to carry out a piece of work, but an appreciation of the overwhelming fatigue that is experienced by some children with

ABI may indicate that to be a significant factor. A summary of the information can be agreed, to include:

- why the behaviour occurs (e.g. Jennifer finds it hard to concentrate)
- the conditions relating to the behaviour, the triggers and the context, i.e. what prompts it (e.g. when Jennifer is asked to do written work in the afternoon). Additional factors are other children around Jennifer who snigger and make faces to one another because of the difficulties she has in class; they enjoy the entertainment value in watching her become increasingly agitated.
- the consequences (e.g. Jennifer gets angry or upset, sometimes cries, and avoids doing the written tasks)
- other factors at school and home (e.g. Jennifer becomes easily frustrated with her homework and gets angry, shouting abuse at her siblings in the evenings when she has homework).

Develop and implement an intervention plan

The team needs to decide how the learning environment can be changed to address the issues, with the focus on proactive strategies. The plan should identify alternative behaviour and this may need to serve the same purpose as the one to be eliminated, e.g. to enable the child to exercise some control or to gain attention. It must also state the positive strategies and supports that need to be put into place. Strategies need to:

- be collectively agreed
- be easy to implement
- be the least intrusive possible
- have a positive impact on the child and all others in the environment.

e.g. Jennifer has a rest after lunch in a designated quiet area.

She changes the place where she sits in most of her classes.

She is provided with short achievable tasks and given frequent encouragement. When her class has written work to complete in the afternoons, Jennifer is given a differentiated worksheet in a multiple-choice format. This eliminates the necessity to generate ideas, which she was having problems with when tired, and to produce written text.

She is provided with a drink and small snack during mid-afternoon break.

She transfers five minutes early between classes, and at the end of the afternoon before the corridors get busy.

School staff and her parents were delighted with the considerable improvements that these changes made to her behaviour, and also her work.

Determine effectiveness of intervention

After implementing agreed strategies, previously gathered information allows judgements to be made about whether a behaviour is changing over time, i.e. whether it is decreasing or increasing. Many behaviours do not change rapidly and systematic recording may be the only way to discern small but gradual changes. These can amount to bigger changes over time and a record can be useful to encourage continued implementation of particular strategies. It is important to seek the opinions of the whole team regarding the effectiveness of the intervention plan and whether it should be continued or a different strategy considered.

Responding to behavioural incidents

It is important to intervene in the setting when and where the behaviours occur. Talking to the child in some other location following a time delay may not be helpful; the child with ABI may have forgotten about a specific incident and also may have difficulties in making a connection between what is being said in one setting and his behaviour in another. However, sometimes it is not possible or appropriate to address a behavioural incident at the time it occurs (see below), in which case it will be necessary to calmly remind the child about the incident, out of the hearing of others, and provide explicit instructions about how he should behave.

Do not ask a child with an ABI to explain the reasons for his inappropriate behaviour, but redirect him. A child or adolescent with ABI, whose behaviour is beyond acceptable limits or is escalating towards this, is not feeling calm or relaxed! Children with ABI show limited self-awareness and have difficulty analysing and monitoring their own behaviour. Their ability to problem solve or to organise their thoughts is even more limited when they are tired or anxious. This will also make it hard for them to recall the events that triggered their inappropriate behaviour, no matter how short the time span. This is not the time to reprimand. Do not argue, or discuss at this point; redirect the child to another activity within the room or, if emotions have been running high, allow the child to go to a quiet place where the level of stimulation is low. This can provide time for him to calm down, free from the stress factors in the classroom. If a reprimand is necessary and the child is already agitated, do this when he is calmer; use a tone of voice that is firm, quiet and devoid of emotion. Make statements rather than ask questions, placing the emphasis on the appropriate behaviour to be displayed under these circumstances, i.e. state exactly what the child must do next time. Avoid non-specific comments such as 'behave yourself' or 'try being good for a change', which give no clues to how a child should behave.

Respond in a calm neutral manner. Maintain eye contact, and use verbal and body language – tone, volume, words, stance, etc. – that are emotive-free. Do not over-react. It is very important that the adults in charge are in control of their own feelings, as any expression of anger or irritability will only serve to increase the child's anxiety and negative reactions.

The least restrictive strategy for managing behaviours must always be used.

Do not simply react to what is observed. Remember that behaviour is a manifestation of other difficulties. It is important to ascertain the reasons for a child's inappropriate response.

Time Out

'Time Out', in behavioural terms, is an extreme form of ignoring a child's inappropriate behaviour where the child is removed for a brief period of time from the group or class to an area which is devoid of stimulation to give opportunity to calm down. It is a non-rewarding strategy and based on the principle that the child will want to return to the usual setting which is more interesting and desirable, and hence will behave in a way that enables a return. Time Out usually means time out from opportunities to be positively rewarded. It is sometimes used as part of a programme for managing very challenging behaviour of children in special settings, some of whom have behaviour difficulties following acquired brain injury, and it has associated implications for resources, safety and the child's well-being and, therefore, needs to be managed very carefully.

The expression 'Time Out' can sometimes be used in a loose way to describe different ways of managing behaviour and so it is important to establish a shared understanding of the term in any context. 'Time Out' should not be confused with the need for children with ABI to have a special place in school where they can go to relax or to calm down, away from the stimulating classroom environment (see below).

Quiet place of rest

Difficulties filtering out the range of stimuli common in busy classrooms and trying to understand and to remember what is expected of them can quickly create a build-up of negative emotions in a child who is struggling to make sense of the situation. A range of factors can lead to behavioural outbursts that represent the child saying, 'this is all too much for me, I can't cope'. Punitive action is not desirable or effective, but the child may well benefit from moving away from a situation which has become overwhelming. It is important that a child with ABI has access to a safe place in which to rest or work at school, which has a low level of stimulation, when the classroom conditions are more demanding than they can manage.

Additional behavioural issues following ABI

Post-traumatic stress disorder (PTSD)

PTSD in children following traumatic brain injury has yet to be extensively studied. There can be a wide range of emotional and physical reactions displayed following any severe traumatic event and PTSD can be experienced by both adults and children. Symptoms such as flashbacks, nightmares or frightening thoughts – especially when exposed to events or objects reminiscent of the trauma – sleep disturbance, depression, anxiety, irritability or anger outbursts may be experienced. PTSD in children with traumatic brain injury is complicated, because many symptoms overlap with those resulting from the brain injury. Central to a diagnosis of PTSD is the re-experiencing or recollection of the event in memory. There is some belief that PTSD and TBI are incompatible because most survivors of TBI have no conscious recollection of the events surrounding their trauma. However, there are increasing indications that PTSD can occur after TBI in children and adolescents (Max *et al.* 1998) and that 'pseudomemories' can have the same impact on emotions as actual ones (Bryant and Harvey 1998). PTSD occurs only rarely and is likely to resolve within months. Pre-existing family problems and the family's reaction to a child's injury may affect the course of PTSD (Crouchman 1998). As previously indicated, there can be a number of factors following ABI that influence strong emotional reactions, such as frustration, anger, sadness, anxiety and depression. They may or may not be related to re-experiencing the traumatic event that resulted in the injury. However, it is important not to dismiss these, whatever the source, and any negative emotional reactions need to be addressed as part of the rehabilitation process.

Denial and lack of self-awareness

Very often children with ABI do not recognise that they have any difficulties as a result of their brain injury, although these can be very obvious to others. They may be unable to appreciate that their behaviour causes offence to adults and peers; they may have unrealistic expectations and anticipate a resumption of their pre-injury lifestyle, despite a range of significant physical or cognitive deficits. Young children can also experience a lack of awareness because of developmental limitations.

Denial and lack of self-awareness are not the same, although frequently the distinction is not made and the terms are used interchangeably. Lack of awareness can be due to a neurological deficit that is a direct result of damage to specific parts of the brain, resulting in an inability to understand. Strictly speaking, denial indicates an awareness of that which is being denied. Denial can be a psychological coping mechanism that serves a very important function of enabling an individual to manage what could otherwise be an overwhelming amount of distressing change. Although this may be healthy during a period of readjustment, long-term denial can be problematic. It can place young people at greater risk of further injury, or abuse, because they do not accept their own vulnerabilities and therefore are unaware of the need for increased safety vigilance. There can be resistance to or a lack of motivation for any additional help or compensatory strategies in school because they do not see the need for any intervention.

Confronting individuals, either parents or children, who experience denial or limited self-awareness is rarely helpful and can lead to even more severe reactions to the injury. Increased awareness of one's own deficits has sometimes been associated with reactions such as substance abuse or depression. Recommendations for working with the issues of denial (Savage and Pearson 1997) are based around opportunities for young people to experience their difficulties as well as their strengths in a supportive environment, with adult help to encourage strategies and consideration about what is needed to experience success, rather than trying to prove that there are problems. Skilful questioning on the part of school staff can enable a young person to focus on strengths and the progress that has been made, and gradually to think about areas that are difficult.

Adolescent Behaviour

Sometimes it can be unclear, particularly to parents, as to what constitutes inappropriate adolescent behaviour. Frequent mood swings, angry outbursts, a lack of co-operation and communication, impulsive behaviour and testing the limits of adult authority are features that can be related to an ABI, but also are not an uncommon feature in adolescence. The mother of a 15-year-old boy who suffered an ABI while mountain biking commented:

> He was going through adolescence before all this and we found it hard going, especially his younger sister who got just as much of his bad behaviour as we did but wasn't old enough to understand the changes in adolescence. Now it is much, much worse. There are arguments every day. He flies off the handle at the slightest thing. We can't get him to co-operate and do any household jobs. We have to make sure he and his sister virtually live separate lives. He doesn't consider anyone else at home except himself and makes demands which, if they're not immediately met, cause him to get into a rage. Life at home as well as at school is so different now and I can't say that any of us are happy. We sometimes ask ourselves if that is how it would have been anyway, even if he hadn't had his accident, or is it because of that?

If there is a known brain injury, it is important to consider the following, adapted from Savage and Pearson (1997):

- Is the behaviour now different in range, intensity and frequency than before the injury?

- Is it different in range, intensity and frequency than that of others of a similar age?
- Does the adolescent seem frustrated?
- Do the problems seem related to memory, attention, initiation and organisation, as well as impulsivity and poor judgement?
- Has the adolescent maintained the same peer group as before the injury?

Reference to current books on adolescence and adolescent behaviour can provide additional information as to what is considered typical development.

Sexual behaviour following ABI

Brain injury can have a direct impact on sexuality, or it may have none at all. An adolescent may experience sexual development that is considered within the typical range; their sexual interests, drive, experiences and socialisation may not be unduly different from those experienced by their peers. Sexuality is thought about and manifested in many different ways, such as in the way individuals create their appearance – their clothes, hair, cosmetics, etc. – how they regard their feminine or masculine persona and how they behave towards others. Adolescence is normally a time associated with increased interest in sex and sexuality and it is not unusual for sexual feelings to be strong in both boys and girls, regardless of a brain injury. Rapid physical and emotional changes and a wish to develop greater autonomy and independence from the family can increase the desire to engage in exciting and risk-taking behaviour. ABI often increases those risks. Physical, cognitive and social changes can disrupt normal sexual maturation and behaviour in a number of different ways:

- Precocious puberty (see Chapter 4).
- Physical deficits can affect a young person's self-image or the way he is viewed by others, or place limitations on his ability to engage in sexual activities.
- Social isolation from peers that frequently occurs after ABI can result in a young person being cut off from what is, for many adolescents, the main source of information about sexual matters.
- Impaired judgement and disinhibition can result in highly inappropriate behaviours including:
  - unwanted, excessive or obsessive sexual comments and innuendoes
  - unwanted touching of another person
  - indiscreet masturbation
  - sexual exploitation either by, or of, others.

Personal, Social and Health Education (PSHE) covers a wide range of topics and the DfES recommends that sex and relationship education should be 'firmly rooted' within the framework for PSHE, and Citizenship Education. Sex education is vital. However, a young person's disinhibited behaviour, and increased vulnerability to abuse or exploitation, are unlikely to be adequately addressed in usual curricular activities. Appropriate sexual behaviour relies on many skills that the adolescent may no longer possess. The power of a sexual drive in someone who has memory difficulties, poor awareness and limited mechanisms for self-control may mean that particular issues or situations require direct and structured intervention in order to minimise risks. School staff and parents need to share any concerns they have and if necessary draw up a behaviour plan. Additional strategies may need to be taught and reinforced on every occasion in which there is heightened risk. (See References section for sources of information that provide more in-depth detail about a range of sexuality issues.)

Depression

School staff must be aware that children, particularly adolescents, with ABI are at increased risk from mental health difficulties following ABI (Max *et al.* 1998). Social skills are highly valued in adolescence and a young person may be aware of his differences and his difficulties in maintaining the kind of social relationships that he used to enjoy and he can become overwhelmed and depressed. Teachers must be alert to changes in behaviour that may indicate depression, such as even greater levels of disorganisation, inattentiveness and isolation; decreased stress threshold; chronic fatigue; crying; mention of suicidal thoughts. Any concerns should be immediately discussed with a relevant clinician so that the child can be evaluated for depression and receive treatment if this is needed.

CHAPTER 8

Social supports

Children with ABI need to have a clear explanation of how their feelings are related to their brain injury, their 'right' to be angry or sad about the changes in themselves, and the confidence that other people understand their problems and will help them surmount their difficulties.

(Savage and Wolcott 1995)

Prior to injury a child or adolescent may have formed some clear concepts of his own identity and personal expectations, acquired through his life experiences and interaction with others, e.g. 'I'm good at sport because I'm on the school football team', 'I have some very good friends; we get together at breaktime and we meet up at weekends'. A sudden loss of skills and abilities can quickly lead to dramatic changes in a child's experiences, which are no longer able to provide confirmation of the self-concepts he may have previously developed. A rapid decline in friendships, social activities or social standing, or perceived 'status' in school, e.g. in terms of academic or sports prowess, can lead to emotional and psychosocial problems, such as lowered self-esteem, social isolation, lack of confidence, and sometimes depression, particularly as many children can remember how they were before their injury. ABI can have a dramatic impact on peer relationships. Loss of friendships are reported by many parents whose children have experienced changes following their ABI – at the very time they desperately need peer contact and support.

Most children learn to understand social cues at an early age. They are commonly learnt intuitively or incidentally, rather than as a result of formal instruction. However, ABI can result in sudden loss of, or problems in using, the knowledge and complex skills involved in social interaction that have been developed over the child's lifetime. Friends who initially offered support after the injury all too frequently drift away. Initiating and maintaining new friendships is problematic. As with many of the behaviour changes after ABI, the social and emotional difficulties are often related to cognitive deficits. Changes to executive functions, in particular, make it hard to process complex social situations. Children with ABI often have little insight into the reasons why their peers no longer choose to interact with them. Also, friends, peers and others commonly lack the skills required to successfully continue a positive relationship with someone who may appear unusual or unpredictable. They often find it difficult to understand how someone with no visible evidence of problems can now be so different.

Difficulties which contribute to social rejection may include:

- Inability to engage effectively in a balanced two-way or group conversation because of disorganised thinking, slow speed of processing information, reduced comprehension and difficulties initiating conversation
- Loss of ability to understand jokes, metaphors or sarcasm, as well as non-verbal communication
- Impulsive, disinhibited behaviour, including 'silly' immature responses
- Invading personal space – standing too close to others or touching them
- Insensitivity to the needs and feelings of others, such as making offensive remarks
- Problems with processing abstract and subtle language.

Social rejection exacerbates a child's difficulties because it precludes opportunities for children to practise social skills that might lead to greater social inclusion.

Many young people with ABI become more dependent on their families for social support and contacts. Studies of young people who have acquired brain injury indicate that significant loneliness is not uncommon. Children who are lonely are at risk of poor adjustment in adult life and at increased risk of getting involved in criminal and delinquent behaviours.

In order to relearn the social skills that a child may have had prior to injury, as well as to develop new skills, it is necessary to assess the deficits first. This cannot be done effectively by psychometric testing or behavioural/social skill rating scales alone. A neuropsychological assessment may indicate deficits in cognitive skills desirable for social success, but the additional environmental factors inherent in social interactions make it essential to include contextual observations, reports and discussions with those who know the child well. It is also important to determine whether the nature of any difficulties stems from a lack of skill acquisition, or problems in using skills which may already have been acquired. There is a distinct difference between the two, and the strategies used to teach desired social skills which are not already part of a child's behavioural repertoire are different from the strategies needed when a child already possesses the skills but fails to use them. For instance, coaching, modelling or direct teaching may be useful approaches for teaching a new skill; reinforcement and motivational strategies may be more relevant if skills have already been learnt.

Five key classroom intervention approaches for helping children who are lonely have been identified by Pavri (2001):

- Social skills training

- Creating opportunities for social interaction
- Creating an accepting classroom climate
- Teaching adaptive coping strategies
- Enhancing children's self-esteem.

The activities mentioned below have been loosely grouped under these approach headings. They have not been devised by the authors, and nor have they been especially designed to use with children with ABI. They have been gathered from a range of sources and have been successfully used with young people with ABI. Any of these kinds of approaches could be included within a PSHE curriculum and can make an important contribution to the development of social supports for all children.

Social skills training

Since the early 1990s there has been a proliferation of social skill training packages, some of which are excellent, and there has been much success in teaching children social skills. The much more difficult task for children with ABI is to learn when and where it is appropriate for them to use the skills. Learning social skills needs to involve a step-by-step approach, augmented by demonstration, role-play, practice and repetition. A child with ABI may have significant difficulties generalising what has been learnt and using this in 'real-life' situations, so it is important that the skills are rehearsed and practised repeatedly in the child's natural environments, i.e. the actual settings in which the skills need to be used. The following strategies may usefully be considered:

- Discuss the rules of interaction regularly. In order for change to occur, a one-off teaching or training period is not enough. Explicit teaching of skills and competencies needs to be ongoing.
- Use positive reinforcement selectively directed to encourage a desired behaviour. Most people respond to compliments and children with ABI should be praised for simple, expected social behaviour that is usually taken for granted in other children.
- Teach specific scripts of common behaviours for situations in which they are frequently expected (e.g. saying good morning; saying please or thank you; giving eye contact to the person who is speaking or is spoken to).
- Encourage imitation of behaviour. Children may learn much about ways to behave by observing and copying someone else's behaviour. This can be a powerful device when the young person identifies with the individual he is aspiring to model, but negative models can be just as highly influential as positive ones. Consideration must be given to the appropriateness of the behaviour demonstrated by the model. The effectiveness will also depend on how motivated the child is to imitate the

behaviours and how much opportunity he has to observe and to practise the desired behaviours. A child will not be influenced by observation if he is unable to remember what he has observed. For this to be used to effect, input is required from an adult who is able to help the child to clearly identify the relevant features that could be copied and for them to be put into practice, rehearsed and repeated in the child's normal settings.

- Consider self-modelling. This is a technique described by Kehle *et al.* (1997) and has been found to be even more effective. This involves the careful filming and editing of the child on video, exhibiting only appropriate behaviours. This can either occur through role-playing and prompting for the purposes of the video, or by recording real situations but editing out inappropriate behaviours. The child is then able to watch his own appropriate behaviour in situations which are problematic for him, with an adult who is instrumental in the behaviour change verbally reinforcing what is seen on video. The pause and replay functions of videos can be helpful for analysing behaviour. Repeated exposure to the information on video and frequent opportunities to practise the behaviours in everyday settings can enhance the learning opportunities. However, extreme caution is required when considering this technique as some children who have experienced significant change, especially visible changes, as a result of an acquired injury and who remember how they were previously, may find video images of their new selves distressing.

Sara suffered a severe traumatic brain injury at the age of 15 when she was in a road traffic accident while travelling by bus on a school outing. After her acute care in a large regional hospital, she was transferred to a residential rehabilitation facility. She made excellent physical and cognitive recovery of many skills. While staying there she enjoyed much attention from her wide extended family, staff, and celebrities who coincidently were visiting the rehabilitation facility at the time she was there. She also received much attention from the local media in her home area, who had taken her cause to heart and were campaigning for safety measures to be put into place on the section of road where the accident occurred. Her school had maintained close contact throughout her absence, making regular visits to see her and sending cards and tapes to remind her of school activities. Her return and early reintegration to school was well supported and successful both academically and socially. She had become quite a celebrity herself! Her friends had been helped to adjust to the changes in Sara, which was considered to contribute to the maintenance of positive peer relationships. About six months after her return, overall progress continued to be very encouraging, but there were reports about the reduction in the quality and quantity of peer interactions. When given opportunity to express their feelings, her peers indicated their considerable irritation about Sara's ongoing expectation to be the centre of attention. They felt that they had made many allowances and adaptations for her after her return and were willing to go on doing so, but they were fed up with the daily behaviours that Sara displayed every time she entered a room whereby she expected to be the centre of attention and to be made a fuss of but never showed an interest in others around her. This issue was very sensitively addressed by her tutor as part of a wider social skills programme in which Sara was involved. Like many of the other subtle social skill difficulties that she now experienced, she was oblivious to the impact of her behaviours on her peers and lacked sensitivity to the needs of others. More desirable behaviour was practised in role-play and then, with Sara's agreement, she was videoed in one of her classrooms so that she could watch herself interacting in a more socially balanced way. She watched this with her tutor on a few occasions and the tape was also used to help demonstrate and teach a number of additional features relating to social communication that Sara had lost. These were part of the normal repertoire of her peers, but were among the factors that 'make her different', as one of them said.

- PATHS (Promoting Alternative Thinking Strategies) is one example of a social skills training package that can have application for children with ABI as well as for a whole primary school approach. It is a process developed in the US by Greenberg and Kusche and reported by Hindley and Reed (1999). It is aimed at promoting the development of the social and emotional skills that underpin social problem solving and was initially devised for use with deaf children, but has been introduced into mainstream primary schools in the UK, for the benefit of all children. It places an emphasis on visual learning materials which, for a child with ABI, can help to augment verbal learning strategies. PATHS covers five areas of social and emotional development: self-control; self-esteem; understanding and recognition of emotions; peer relations; social problem-solving skills.

Creating opportunities for social interaction

Generally children can be very supportive when they are given accurate information to help them to understand the changes in their classmate and are allowed to help problem solve. Without information, peers can be confused and lack the skills to communicate with someone who does not fit into their perceived 'norm'. They, too, need to be provided with new, additional skills or else they will withdraw their communication efforts. However, group strategies are ones that enable all children to benefit. Members of school staff have a critical role to play in providing a supportive environment, where children do not feel that they may be rebuffed or ridiculed if they get it wrong. The following strategies may be useful.

Buddy systems

Buddies are peer helpers with whom the child can be paired up to help provide an informal support network. A 'buddy' needs to be a good role model, who is supportive, tolerant and empathic and who has volunteered to 'look out' for the child during more unstructured times – e.g. break and lunchtimes; on the school bus; transitions between classes – or who sometimes helps to carry books and other materials. There needs to be more than one assigned buddy, and a 'Circle of Friends' (see below) may be a preferable option. Alternatively, buddies may be assigned for particular tasks, e.g. a 'study buddy'. It is essential that none of the volunteers feel a burden of responsibility. They also need to know that they can discuss any concerns they have about their role with an identified member of staff on a regular basis. Buddies may need particular guidance in knowing how to respond to unusual or unexpected behaviours that can occur with children who have an ABI.

Circle of Friends

A Circle of Friends – not to be confused with Circle Time – is something that is often taken for granted by those who have one. Children with ABI all too often lack this kind of supportive network. For a child who does not have a natural circle of friends, a social support network can be created by members of school staff who facilitate the circle process. 'Circle of Friends' is a strategy devised by Pearpoint *et al.* (1996), in which a network of peers choose to develop and maintain a friendship group that supports the notion of acceptance and mutual benefit and includes the child who lacks social contacts. Members of the friendship circle may look out for the child with ABI at breaktimes, transfer classes with him, go to school, attend out of school activities with him, etc. The process is one that can develop from a whole-class activity on the topic of friendship, discussing the nature of friendship and the perceptions and feelings of children who have few or no friends.

Friendship stop

This has been established in the playground of some schools and is a place where any child can go to sit. Children are 'primed' to keep an eye on the stop and to include any child there in their own activity or just to go and chat with them. Some schools have children who volunteer to be on a rota in order to monitor the Friendship Stop. Schools 'set the scene' with explanations to ensure that no one feels different or stigmatised by using it, helping children to understand that many of them will experience some playtimes or situations that are difficult and a Friendship Stop is a facility for everyone in the school who wishes to use it.

Community participation

Actively encourage the child to be involved with youth groups in the local community, the nature of which will depend on interests and access skills. A young person with ABI may try to cling onto the belief that he continues to be part of the same social group of which he was a part prior to his injury, but this may no longer be the case. He may benefit from help to understand that friendships come and go, and that making new connections can provide him with new possibilities.

Consultation

Consulting with parents can help teachers develop a deeper understanding of the social and emotional difficulties a child may be experiencing. Collaboration is also useful to identify out of school activities that may be appropriate for the child.

Creating an accepting classroom climate

Teachers play an important part in developing classroom and wider school environments that nurture a sense of belonging, where children can feel respected and where there is acceptance of difference and diversity.

A useful strategy towards promotion of this is Circle Time. This is based on the principle of everyone in a school community learning to listen to one another, to take responsibility and to work towards a positive school ethos. Jenny Mosley (1999), the author of a number of books on Circle Time, emphasises that it is 'no good creating oases of respect in the classroom...if the other policies do not also foster and ensure respect for both children and adults'. She has devised a 'Whole School Quality Circle Time Model', which is aimed at meeting the needs of all individuals in the school. A Whole School Quality Circle Time approach includes the provision for the times of the school day when specific difficulties are most likely to occur, e.g. lunch and playtimes can be problematic because of their unstructured nature. Circle Time can involve the teaching of playground games, the provision of playground zones supervised by older children, and activities for children who need more structure.

Teaching adaptive coping strategies

The predominant issue of loss, already referred to, is one that is extremely hard for a child to adjust to without help. It is not surprising that children with ABI are often affected by emotional disturbance because of all the changes to their life and lifestyle. Opportunities for regular counselling can provide a way of assisting a young person to manage the difficulties he perceives as well as being a safe setting in which to express his feelings. He may benefit from having an opportunity to discuss fears, worries, relationships, sexuality and other intimate issues, free from fear of disclosure to peers, parents or other school staff. A range of counselling approaches may need to be considered and Lehr (1997) emphasises the importance of tailoring the interventions to the child's skills and changing needs. The focus may be, for example, on managing conflict, understanding the changes that have occurred, planning for transitions, making new friends, etc. Individual counselling may be what is required at a particular time, but group, family or sibling counselling may also be useful to consider.

Unfortunately most people who offer counselling services do not have any training or experience in working with children and adolescents with ABI. It is essential that anyone who offers this kind of support acquaints themselves with the core issues of ABI and the deficits and limitations of the individual child in order to maximise opportunities to communicate effectively. The adult in a counselling role must have appreciation of why a child with ABI may respond differently from a child with a brain that is neurologically intact.

It is important that young people with ABI have an identified member of school staff with whom they can link up at least once a day. Ideally this should be someone with whom the young person feels he has a positive relationship. This person can assess how well the youngster is coping by meeting with him daily and gathering observations from other school staff.

Enhancing children's self-esteem

MAPs (Making Action Plans), which is devised and described by Pearpoint *et al.* (1996), is a collaborative planning process that involves the 'key actors' in a child's life. The child, the child's family, any particular peers, teachers and other significant people meet and discuss the child's and the family's personal dreams and goals, and together they think of ways of making them a reality, by drawing up an action plan and following it through. The key issue that is addressed is: What does the child and family want? This is a powerful process because it involves the people who are already key figures in the child's life, collaborating and negotiating specific steps to create and affect a plan of action.

CHAPTER 9

Individual education planning and provision

The educational experience can be more appropriate if educators take individual differences into account, analyze the learning tasks that must be accomplished, determine those student behaviors that contribute to success or non-success, create a learning environment conducive to the student's needs and selectively apply a variety of teaching techniques and strategies.

(Blosser and DePompei 1994)

As previously explained, the special educational needs of children with acquired brain injuries are frequently complex, sometimes not easy to identify and generally different in nature or in combination from those of other children with special needs. This, therefore, presents a challenge for those planning to meet these needs in schools.

Although we are all aware that the identification of needs for each child should be considered on a very individual basis, when looking at Individual Education Plans from a range of schools, it is apparent that similar descriptions of need and non-specific expressions of intervention can frequently be seen. This may be understandable if children have difficulties about which members of staff are more aware – for instance, specific learning difficulties such as dyslexia – as they may be familiar with what is required without very specific descriptions. However, the difficulties faced by children with ABI can be open to misinterpretation and often require unique and explicit programmes of intervention.

It is important for parents to be reassured that those experienced in working with children who have SEN for other reasons, and many who do not have this specific expertise, will have the skills necessary to devise and oversee appropriate programmes for children with ABI. However, they will need:

- information regarding ABI, with guidance regarding the most common manifestations of potential difficulties; and
- specific information regarding the individual child in question. Detailed information regarding assessment and identification of these needs is included in Chapter 6, but immediate information can also be sought from the child's parents

and from medical and therapy staff or clinical psychologists who may have been involved with the child.

Individual Education Plans (IEPs) should only be created when a child needs *different* or *additional* intervention from that which the school normally provides within the differentiated, inclusive curriculum. As the pattern of difficulties that children demonstrate following ABI is different from other children with SEN, it is most likely that this will apply to them. As their needs are different from others, it is unlikely that a group IEP will be appropriate.

Planning for provision

Comparison with other children

Sometimes it may seem that these children do not have significant additional needs. Teachers often comment that there are other children in the class with much greater levels of difficulty, for whom intervention under School Action or School Action Plus may seem to be more clearly indicated. Quite understandably, as there are enough demands on teachers towards meeting diverse needs within an inclusive curriculum, they do not want to create additional concerns or burdens when these are unnecessary. However, as the child with ABI is likely to have some preserved areas of ability in addition to his acquired problems and a store of previously acquired knowledge and skills, he may well have considerably more potential than he can demonstrate without additional support and resources. His overall achievements may not be significantly worse than some of his peers, but it is only relevant to compare these children with their previous and current potential, not with other pupils.

John was six years old when he suffered a traumatic brain injury in a road traffic accident. Three years later he was achieving at a very low level in school, but no particular concerns were raised and he was not in receipt of any significant additional support or resources. The head teacher insisted that he had no particular difficulties and had no acquired problems as a result of the accident. He said that his level of ability and concentration were in line with that of his siblings and even said that he had taught John's father years previously and that they were similar. The class teacher said that John never concentrated well, rarely completed tasks without prompts and that they joked in class that he was a 'daydreamer' and she and the other children often called to him to come back to Planet Earth! John laughed with them about this.

Investigation revealed that John has post-traumatic epilepsy and was suffering from absence seizures. He also has other significant acquired attentional problems in addition to difficulties with organisation and initiation. When these were recognised and addressed, his achievements increased significantly.

John's academic performance was no worse than some of his peers, nor did he present as a child with behavioural difficulties. No specific difficulties were identified when he was compared with other children, but with the knowledge of his acquired brain injury his performance was considered in a different light, which enabled his difficulties to be recognised and therefore addressed.

Prediction of needs

It is important to realise that ABI frequently does provoke learning difficulties, although not necessarily apparent ones when the child first returns to school. Many children like John do not appear to have significant needs at Key Stages 1 and 2, but their difficulties – and the differences between them and their peers – become much more pronounced as they progress through the education system. This can provoke much more significant learning and, sometimes, behavioural difficulties, as a result of prolonged failure and frustration or changes in demands during Key Stages 3 and 4. These can be avoided if difficulties are accepted and addressed as early as possible. Comparisons can be made here with children with developmental dyslexia with whom most teachers are now familiar. Sousa (2001) also refers to children in schools with 'dual exceptionality':

> whose abilities and disabilities mask each other. They... are considered average students, and do not seem to have any problems or any special needs. Although they may seem to be performing well, they are in fact functioning well below their potential. In later high school years, as course work becomes more difficult, learning difficulties may become apparent, but their true potential will not be realized.

Too often, when a child returns to school following an acquired brain injury and seems to be making such a good recovery, a 'wait and see' policy is adopted. However, with an awareness of the potential effects of such an injury, it is not reasonable to expect him to reintegrate, without considering how this injury may affect his access to the curriculum and his potential.

David was said to have made a 'remarkable' recovery from a serious TBI. He returned to his mainstream Key Stage 2 placement with no specific additional support/differentiation. He was initially referred for a statutory assessment of his special educational needs, but the school's educational psychologist then recommended withdrawal of this request when he tested David and found that he had regained age-appropriate levels of achievement. He soon transferred to Key Stage 3 and began to show increasing difficulties with work and, more particularly, with behaviour. His behaviour was addressed by methods which were used for other children. This was unsuccessful and David was permanently excluded. He transferred to a special school and his needs were considered in the same way as the other pupils with learning difficulties. This was not successful. Eventually he faced the possibility of permanent exclusion again, but additional non-teaching assistance was provided in order for him to remain in school. However, his individual needs resulting from his brain injury were still not considered and this also failed. David withdrew from school before the end of Year 10.

David has the intellectual ability for achievement at GCSE and if there had been an early understanding of his *different* difficulties and the challenges that he would face as he continued through school, he may have had greater opportunity to realise his ability and to maximise his progress. As it was, his behavioural and psychological difficulties compounded and increased.

'Invisible' deficits

Damage caused in acquired brain injury is not visible. If the child had suffered permanent damage to an area of the body, such as his dominant hand, the problem would be immediately addressed and assumptions would not be made that he would 'cope'. Comments regarding the fact that there were other children in the class who were also clumsy would not be made. No one would wait to see if not being able to write appropriately affected his educational potential or caused him problems before planning intervention. When targets were set for him, this would not be with the expectation that he could 'fix' his hand. 'To learn how to use his right hand to write legibly and at an appropriate speed' would not be set as a realistic target. If there was the possibility that he could regain some use of this with appropriate training or exercises, this may be incorporated into his programme, but in the meantime alternative means would be found to enable him to record his work. He would be provided with any necessary additional resources, along with training and support, in order for him to be able to use these efficiently. There should be no lesser consideration of injury to the brain and the loss or impairment of specific skills that it controls.

Compensatory strategies

As these children have permanent deficits resulting from their injuries, some provision should then focus on the development of compensatory strategies. An example of this could be a memory impairment. Some people have better memories than others and there is, therefore, a significant range of potential within the normal population. However, teachers generally expect children to be able to make more effort; to work harder; or to find ways of remembering information, for instance for tests or exams. Assumptions are made that some children do not spend enough time revising and, therefore, lack motivation or commitment. However, if his ability to remember is permanently impaired, regardless of how much time the child spends trying to remember information in the way that his friends do and in the way that he used to, he will be unsuccessful. A teacher telling him to try harder is unhelpful at best and frustrating and provocative at worst. He needs to relearn different ways of maximising his ability and to have support to compensate for his deficits.

Gaps in educational progress

Even if a child has made subsequent improvement following an ABI, there may be gaps in the 'building blocks' necessary for future learning because of time in hospital and away from school and levels of cognitive difficulties. It is important to think about the 'gaps' in a child's education since his injury: gaps in experiential and direct learning; gaps in achievement; and gaps in social skills development and interpersonal relationships. It may be necessary to address skills or information that his peers have covered in previous years or key stages.

Cognitive styles

Much has been written recently relating to 'brain-based' learning and cognitive styles. Individuals process and learn information in a variety of ways. For instance, Smith (2002) points out that 'Albert Einstein said numerical ideas came to him more or less as images that he could combine at will, whereas others have said they rely on verbal representations of numbers when thinking about problems.'

Issues relating to cognitive style are particularly important to consider in terms of the changes that may be faced by a child with ABI. It is difficult for anyone to change preferred styles of learning, revising, remembering, etc., but acquired difficulties affecting specific skills may necessitate this, as previous styles may no longer be efficient. Information regarding cognitive styles often refers to specific models of learning used by different people, within which children with ABI may no longer fit. They may demonstrate an unusual combination or confusion of styles requiring more careful interpretation or analysis and encouragement of appropriate learning strategies.

Identification of needs

It is important initially to focus away from preconceived ideas regarding the difficulties faced by other children and the interventions normally appropriate for them. When considering the specific needs of children with ABI, information should be obtained from relevant teaching and non-teaching staff and, if appropriate, brief observation of the child. As referred to in Chapter 6, the questions when? where? and why? may be useful to ask in relation to difficulties that are identified. For instance, if a child has widespread difficulties with concentration, or specific problems with reading, it is essential to consider if his performance is better or worse at different times, in different environments, or with different activities, etc.

It is helpful to consider what skills he needs in order to be able to complete a specific task, e.g.

- What skills does he need to be able to concentrate/to be able to read?
- Does he have some of these, but lack others?
- Do certain situations/environments/instructions enable him to achieve more?

Each curricular area and each activity within it will require a slightly different combination of underlying skills to enable the child to succeed. For instance, it is clear that different combinations of skills – controlled by different areas of the brain – are necessary in Maths depending on whether the task involves: 'mechanical' computations; numerical reasoning; geometry; estimation; data handling; algebra; rote learning of tables, etc.

Approach to the identification of problem areas must be analytical to enable appropriate target setting and intervention planning. Once a teacher begins to consider the skills necessary to complete a task, problem areas often become apparent. It then can be clear why the child can complete one task but not another, which superficially seem comparable, or can work in one environment but not another. The following checklist may serve to instigate this analytical process, although teachers may well add to or adapt this. Does the child demonstrate the following skills necessary for efficient learning at an age-appropriate level?

Ability to:

- attend to verbal and visual information
- ignore a reasonable level of distractions
- shift attentional focus
- multi-task to an age-appropriate level
- show persistence to complete a task
- generalise information or skills from one situation to another
- adapt to changes of routine
- process incoming information at an age-appropriate rate
- complete oral or written tasks at an age-appropriate rate
- retain information in working memory
- retain information in long-term memory
- retrieve information from memory
- problem solve to an age-appropriate level
- display appropriate motivation
- sequence tasks or activities
- display efficient visuo-perceptual ability to: interpret information from within a complex page or background; recognise, match and differentiate visual symbols in literacy, numeracy, etc.

- display efficient visual ability (with or without aids)
- indicate adequate hearing ability
- scan visual information efficiently
- display age-appropriate abstract reasoning
- demonstrate flexible thinking
- efficiently interpret social and non-verbal cues and behaviours
- be aware of own strengths and weaknesses
- retain an overview (not become lost in details)
- initiate activities
- inhibit inappropriate actions or impulsive behaviours
- express information verbally
- express information in writing
- retrieve appropriate vocabulary for verbal and written communication
- display fine motor and pencil control skills (or alternatives with appropriate technology)
- display efficient motor planning skills
- display appropriate gross motor skills.

Differentiation

In order to meet the needs of a child with ABI, it is important to remember that there may be a need for differentiation of any of the following:

- teaching methods
- curricular content
- materials
- environments
- expectations.

Information relating to specific strategies and provision is detailed in Chapter 10.

Individual Education Plans

Individual Education Plans must be useful, practical documents to assist teachers' planning. Ideally they will be devised with the involvement of parents, along with appropriate teaching staff and the school's SENCO.

They should include information regarding *what* should be taught, *how* it should be taught and *how often* it should be taught. For many children with ABI, the most important things that they need to learn in order to access the curriculum and to make academic progress are:

- Strategies to overcome some of their acquired deficits (e.g. relating to memory)
- New approaches to learning to take into account current strengths and weaknesses
- Some specific skills that develop intuitively in children without brain injury, which may have to be explicitly taught to these children (e.g. some communication or planning skills).

Teaching of these skills may need to be on an individual basis. Depending on the nature and complexity of the child's difficulties, this could be undertaken by either a teacher or a teaching assistant (TA), under the direction of a teacher. It is very important that even though these skills may be taught and practised at specific times, they should be reinforced and prompted in all areas of the curriculum.

Formulating targets

The targets for these children may relate, for instance, to improving academic achievement in literacy or numeracy, but also to improvements in underlying skills or behaviour. The latter can easily be formulated as **SMART targets** (specific, measurable, achievable, relevant and time bound).

When targets are set for a child with ABI it is important to consider terminology. Before formulating targets with the onus on the child for improvement, thought must first be turned to the identified cause of the problem and consideration given to what is achievable. If the child has impaired attentional ability he cannot improve this at will. However, with more of an onus on school staff to provide means by which he can *maximise* his impaired attention a target can be made appropriate. This should not absolve the child of responsibility to work towards his goals once he has been provided with the appropriate resources, strategies and opportunities to do this, but it does recognise his underlying disability. Targets should be clear, informative and unambiguous to *all* those who come into contact with the child.

Identifying and understanding the underlying disability that causes the child's difficulties is the best way of minimising some of the disabling effects of ABI. Addressing the root causes of the problem is generally successful in enabling the child to maximise his potential, e.g.

> **why** is he slow to develop early reading skills?
> **why** is Maths difficult?
> **why** can he not understand concepts of turn taking?

The child with ABI may be seen to have difficulties or special needs in a relatively large number of areas. However, it is not appropriate to attempt to meet too many targets at one time, as this is too confusing for both the child and the staff. Identifying causes as well as manifestations can help to address a number of issues at the same time. However, if necessary, issues must be prioritised in order of importance.

Planning intervention

Many suitable strategies and methods will already be familiar to teachers of children with special educational needs. The difference is that they may not be used to utilising them with children presenting unusual profiles of strengths and difficulties, e.g. some strategies used for children with moderate or specific learning difficulties may never be considered for a more able child. However, a small steps approach may be necessary or implementation of strategies used for working with children with dyslexia may be useful.

Some of these children may also benefit from specific peer support or involvement of a counsellor or mentor. This needs careful planning, however, and is referred to in Chapter 8.

Success criteria

Once underlying problems are identified, work towards ameliorating or compensating for those becomes the focus for the IEP, rather than curricular issues. The targets and methods, therefore, change but the success criteria can still relate to the curriculum. For instance, if an underlying difficulty relating to attentional skills is identified, maximising this ability could be a target, ways of attempting to achieve this could be agreed, but the measure of success could be in terms of time spent on specific curricular tasks, such as numeracy or literacy.

Reviews

Once an initial plan detailing appropriate intervention has been agreed, it is important to review this after a shorter time than would normally be considered. This is partly because these children's needs are often complex and require different types or combinations of approaches which need more careful initial monitoring to evaluate their efficacy. The needs of children with ABI also often change more frequently than for children with other learning difficulties. If targets have not been met there must be consideration at the review of the appropriateness of both the target and the intervention. It may be that one or both of these requires revision.

Teaching assistants

Although recommendations in the current Code of Practice are that additional assistance for a child in school should not immediately be viewed in terms of personnel

– usually teaching assistants – this is often what is considered by schools and LEAs.

As suggested within the Code, consideration should be given to other resources – including in-service training, non-contact time for teachers to plan and to prepare materials and IT resources – and *not* just to the provision of a laptop computer. However, there is also a valuable and useful role for teaching assistants.

Many teaching assistants are extremely dedicated and experienced, but some have lacked the support and training they seek to enable them to fulfil their role to the best of their ability. Hopefully, this should change as a result of current programmes of improved training and qualifications for school support staff, backed by government funding. TAs cannot be in a position to support students with ABI effectively without appropriate awareness raising and supervision.

The specific role and responsibilities of a TA in this respect should be clearly defined and justified.

The child with ABI may need:

- additional repetition and reinforcement of key information or skills to be mastered
- simplification of some verbally presented information
- presentation of certain information or instructions on an individual basis
- extra time to complete activities or pieces of work
- differentiation of written or visually presented information
- a quiet environment to work on certain tasks or to learn key facts
- provision of additional visual organising aids
- provision of verbal or visual cues or prompts
- practice at using strategies to compensate for impairments of, for instance, memory or organisational skills
- work within an individual programme towards improving specific skills for learning
- practice of, and assistance with, IT skills
- physical help or supervision for certain practical tasks
- practice within a programme devised by an appropriate therapist
- someone to provide a key point of contact between home and school
- planned practice of social skills within a small group.

All of these areas of need may be met by a teaching assistant working under supervision, with a clearly defined role and to a prepared programme of intervention.

The keys to appropriate use of such an assistant are:

- efficient and clear initial assessment and planning – a good IEP
- appropriate consideration of timetabling and curricular breadth

- training and awareness raising for the assistant
- clearly defined role and goals
- adequate support and supervision
- provision of advance information from teachers
- adequate preparation time for the TA.

Assessment and planning

Reference has been made previously to the fact that accurate identification of the child's needs is important. A TA allocated to work with a child with ABI will need these to be clearly defined and stated. The agreed strategies to address these must also be clear and unambiguous.

Timetabling and curriculum

If the TA is to spend some time working individually with the child to address topics on an individual basis or to reinforce work or topics previously covered, careful consideration of the timetable must take place. This intervention will need to be conducted at an appropriate time and place – not at one end of the staffroom during assembly, or at the end of the day if the child suffers from fatigue. It may be appropriate to consider reducing the number of curricular subjects in order to increase achievement and meaningful learning in other, selected ones.

Training

If a TA is to work extensively or on a long-term basis with a child with ABI, he should have access to appropriate information and training relating to the child's condition. This will be in addition to any other training and personal development work encouraged and planned for teaching assistants in general. As with teachers, there is nothing in the training towards qualifications for this job that relates to acquired brain injury.

Role definition

The expectations of TAs are often complex and demanding. It will be rare for this to include doing anything exclusively on behalf of the child; there are some instances when TAs are required to take notes or to write ones that the child dictates, but even this should not occur without prior thought and consideration of the reasons for this. Most often the TA will be assisting or enabling the child to access the curriculum by differentiation, repetition, rehearsal, etc., or by facilitating him to develop strategies to maximise his own potential

Supervision

However good a teaching assistant is and however experienced, he is not a teacher. Plans to ensure that teaching assistants receive better training in general or specific areas of their work and to encourage them to strive for recognition of Higher Level Teaching Assistant status (HLTA) do not remove the responsibility from teachers for supervision and whole-curricular planning. As stated in the National Agreement on School Workforce Reforms: 'we recognise that accountability for the overall learning outcomes of a particular pupil must rest with the pupil's assigned qualified teacher. Teachers and higher-level teaching assistants are not interchangeable' (DfES 2003). All TAs should have regular support and supervision by appropriate teaching staff, who should review and monitor their work.

Advance information

A key role for TAs is often to produce differentiated visual or written material. This may just involve photocopying worksheets etc. in order to cut and paste the information onto separate sheets in more manageable amounts. It may involve enlarging diagrams or illustrations, removing them from the body of text, or using alternative labelling. It may involve adding additional headings, lists of key words or highlighting sections. In order to do this, the assistant will require copies of the material from the teacher in advance.

Sometimes, if a significant proportion of the information or instructions in a lesson are to be provided orally, a TA may need to remove a child with poor attentional or language comprehension skills to a quiet area during this time and present the information in an alternative manner and environment. In order to plan this, the TA will require notification of lesson content in advance.

Preparation time

Having received information from staff and being aware of other material that the child requires, e.g. organisational aids, the TA must have sufficient non-contact time to prepare.

Working co-operatively

As previously mentioned, the role of the TA within a classroom is a challenging one, but so is the role of the teacher when working with and supervising a TA. As more TAs are now employed within schools, teachers are increasingly familiar with this role, but some still find this difficult and can be uncomfortable establishing an appropriate working relationship. It is important for the two adults to have mutual respect and understanding of each other's roles and for the teacher to be confident to supervise and to direct the assistant when necessary. The teacher must respect the assistant's knowledge of the child and his difficulties and of the programme that has been agreed for him. It is appropriate for training to be provided for teachers regarding working with teaching assistants as well as for the assistants themselves.

CHAPTER 10

Classroom strategies

Rehabilitation and education professionals agree that good teaching strategies designed especially for students with ABI are necessary and essential.

(Blosser and DePompei 1994)

There are many well-established methods of working with children with special educational needs that are very appropriate to incorporate into programmes for those with acquired brain injuries. Some strategies for pupils with a range of difficulties, such as developmental dyslexia or dyspraxia, autistic spectrum disorders or ADHD may be relevant, but adaptations will obviously be necessary to suit each child's individual profile of needs.

The following is not a comprehensive list, but provides ideas and suggestions, already 'tried and tested' in classrooms, that may be useful to consider for children with ABI. School staff may be able to think of many other suggestions to assist the particular young people with whom they are working. Decisions to use any of the following should only be made in the light of knowledge of an individual child's strengths and difficulties.

Physical and sensory

Gross motor difficulties

- Obtain advice from a physiotherapist
- Allow sufficient time/space for activities
- Establish protocol for negotiating crowded places
- Provide help for carrying objects.

Fine motor difficulties

- Obtain advice from an occupational therapist
- Consider alternative methods of recording work – not necessarily a laptop computer
- Provide support and/or adapted materials in practical subjects
- Provide grips for writing implements
- Provide clips or non-slip surfaces for stabilising writing paper
- Provide roller or gel pens for writing

Ataxia or tremor

- Ensure good sitting posture when working: chair and table at correct height; sitting 'square' to the table; feet flat on the floor; elbows/forearms on the work surface; leant slightly forwards
- Allow child to sit rather than stand when appropriate

Visual difficulties

- Ask parents to provide information from any treating ophthalmologist or optician
- Obtain advice from specialist LEA support services
- Ensure optimal seating and lighting
- Use markers or guides to assist tracking when reading
- Provide high contrast for visual information
- Prompt the wearing of spectacles if prescribed
- Establish class rules for 'clutter-free' room
- Determine optimal font size for text
- Allow extra time to complete tasks

Hearing difficulties

- Ask parents to provide information from any treating audiologist
- Obtain advice from specialist LEA support services
- Ensure optimal seating for listening
- Make eye contact when speaking to the child
- Minimise background noise
- Provide written information to accompany verbal instructions
- Ensure videos are subtitled or prepare notes in advance

Headaches

- Establish protocol with parents/carers regarding use of analgesia etc.
- Provide drinking water
- Monitor pattern, duration, severity, frequency of headaches and contact home if there are any changes
- If occurring at specific times (e.g. every Maths lesson) don't assume the cause to be an avoidance strategy; also consider other factors such as environmental. e.g. task difficulties, lighting, noise, etc.

Fatigue

- Graded return to school/time at school after injury
- Timetable most-demanding tasks at optimum performance times if possible
- Provide breaks/rest periods
- Remember having a snack or meal can help
- A 'buddy' to carry books and equipment between classroom changes
- Develop a strategy to use when fatigue is obvious (e.g. a designated quiet area for ten minutes)
- Reduce demands when appropriate – do not insist on continuation/completion of a task
- Discuss management of homework with staff, parents and pupil – is it necessary?
- Consider extra time in exams
- Reduce demands when appropriate

Epilepsy

- Obtain appropriate information from parents/carers regarding the nature of the child's epilepsy
- Find out if there is a dedicated epilepsy nurse at your local hospital to provide advice, or ask the school nurse
- When a child has a seizure, remain calm and do not over-react
- Follow published guidelines for managing seizures
- Ensure an area is available for the child to rest after seizures if necessary
- Keep a record of the times and duration of seizures and inform parents
- If a child with ABI shows unexpected inattention/daydreaming, inform his parents and suggest they mention it at the child's next medical appointment
- If a child is taking anti-convulsant medication, report any increased tiredness, slowness or deterioration in school work to his parents, particularly if his medication has just been changed or increased

Language and communication

Word-finding difficulties

- If initial sound cues help, give these unless the child finds this embarrassing
- Prompt with whole words if this is acceptable to the child
- Provide a list of key words for specific topics
- Use multiple-choice assessment whenever possible

Language organisation difficulties

- Produce pro forma to structure work
- Provide headings, bullet points or key words
- Use software and other resources designed for dyslexics to aid organisation

Slow language processing

- Provide as much information as possible in advance of lessons (e.g. next lesson we will be discussing volcanoes on page X of the textbook)
- Allow as much extra time as possible for completion of work
- Repeat instructions in a different order
- Whenever possible, provide short instructions or pieces of information interspersed by gaps
- Provide written backup for verbal information/instructions

Language comprehension difficulties

- Simplify and rephrase instructions and information
- Provide verbal and written information in smaller amounts – 'chunking'
- Specifically teach skills to search for and extract information/meaning from text
- Provide any questions prior to the child reading text
- Assess his reading comprehension as well as his word recognition skills
- Provide a quiet environment at key times to encourage understanding of important information
- Ask the child to explain what he has been told in his own words to check understanding
- Do not use sarcasm
- Explain things directly – not by inference
- Provide summaries of complicated or obtuse text
- Encourage choice of less language-based subjects at Key Stage 4 and beyond

Written language difficulties

- Allow alternative methods of recording (e.g. audio tapes, IT, etc.)
- Highlight areas of the page that are ignored or confused
- Reduce amounts to be read and provide some parts verbally
- Present written information in small sections
- Place a piece of dark card over a page with a 'window' cut out so that the child can concentrate on just one part at a time
- Provide a quiet environment at key times to encourage production of important information

Attention

Sustained attention difficulties

- Use frequent changes of task whenever possible
- Allow brief breaks within a task
- Consider when important information is conveyed. Try to ensure that this is at the beginning of a lesson or after a brief break, or that it is repeated at these times
- Give explicit instructions for what the child should be doing, avoiding commands such as 'pay attention'
- Be aware of 'attentional drift' and redirect the child (e.g. by making eye contact, saying name or lightly touching)

Selective attention difficulties (distractibility)

- Allow quiet environments for specific, selected activities
- Reinforce specific information in a quiet environment if necessary (e.g. with TA)
- Remove distractors from immediate working environment
- Seek the child's undivided attention before speaking or instructing

Dividing attention difficulties

- Avoid need for multi-tasking:
- Give out handouts when information is being provided orally or when dictating
- Allow recording of orally presented information to enable note taking at a later stage
- Allow the child to stop working when he is being spoken to or receiving further instructions

Shifting attention difficulties

- Give advance warning of change of activity whenever possible
- Allow 'settling down' time at the beginning of lessons
- Try not to give out important information or set complicated tasks at the beginning of lessons, or repeat it again later

Memory

Working memory difficulties

- Provide prompt sheets and visual cues
- Categorise information or instructions to provide links
- Write down instructions
- Use graphic or other visual organisers/*aides-mémoire* for frequently required tasks/activities

Long-term storage and recall difficulties

- Repetition, repetition, repetition! in different formats, situations, etc.
- Make information meaningful for the child
- Link new information to previously known facts
- Practise remembering; the need to recall information on a number of occasions will assist encoding
- Use different modalities (e.g. multisensory work as with dyslexics)
- Provide cues to aid recall
- Use multiple-choice formats whenever possible
- Put questions in context and link with other information with which it was originally learnt
- Encourage use of memory aids (e.g. diary, homework planner)
- Use mnemonics and visualisation techniques
- Use flow charts and mind-mapping techniques

Information processing

Slow information- and language-processing speed

- Allow more time for responses whenever possible
- Allow additional time to complete work
- Prompt when necessary – verbally or with provision of written/visual list – to reinforce lists of tasks
- Remember that significant amounts of information may have been missed
- Control amount of information that the child is to work with at any one time
- Set appropriate targets for quantity of work
- Modify expectations regarding homework and exams

Perception/Sensation

Over-sensitivity to stimuli

- Seek advice from an occupational therapist
- Be aware of the child's difficulties and make allowances for extreme reactions
- Inform peers of his difficulties as appropriate
- Arrange appropriate environments for times when concentration is particularly important

Other difficulties with sensory integration

- Seek advice from a specialist occupational therapist

Spatial skill difficulties

- Use pro forma or tables to assist setting out work
- Use very visible 'markers' in the physical environment
- Ensure safety in school and on outside visits
- Provide additional exercises with, for instance, positions and patterns
- Be aware of the difficulties and provide additional time/assistance when addressing relevant curricular areas (e.g. symmetry in Maths or work in DT)

Other visuo-perceptual difficulties

- Use books with clear, well-spaced text
- Additional work regarding matching, identification of shapes – including words – in pictures, text, local environment, etc.
- Use of consistent format for important text
- Practise with visual, strategic searches
- Sorting activities (at any level)
- Simplification of visually presented material
- Highlighting of important information
- Use dark card or paper with 'windows' to reveal only small pieces of text at one time

Executive functioning

Planning and organising difficulties

- Calendar or diary to list dates for work to be handed in
- Extra assistance for time planning for work at Key Stages 3 and 4
- Child to compile a daily 'to do' list
- Use daily planner and timetable
- Provide the first steps of a sequence for the child to complete
- Visual organisers (e.g. step-by-step checklist of components of task or tasks for the child to cross off/remove/erase as completed)
- Uncluttered work area
- Limit number of steps in a task
- Encourage the child to think of next steps in task (e.g. 'Good, now what will you do next?')
- 'Advance organisers', i.e. information to help child with task prior to starting it (e.g. discuss and provide outline of task, key points, and purpose of task)

Problem-solving difficulties

- Reinforce problem solving in different curricular areas (e.g. what is the problem? ways of solving problem; think of several ways, plus pros and cons of each one; identify best solution; create a plan of action; evaluate this)
- Use problems that the child has experienced and discuss alternative strategies
- Encourage the child to think about alternatives and consequences

Self-monitoring difficulties

- Use a 'traffic light' analogy and visual aid to help the child stop and think, 'Am I doing what I should be doing?'
- Teach the child to look for clues from others as to appropriateness of behaviour (e.g. 'reading' facial expressions that suggest disapproval)
- Agree a prompt to indicate inappropriate behaviour

Initiation difficulties

- Provide an agreed signal – which the child decides – to act as a reminder to start a task
- Have very clear, visual and simple plan in the child's work area (e.g. Goal – Plan – Do)
- Incorporate a fun or novel element into stages of the task
- Provide steps of the task one at a time so as not to overwhelm the child
- Praise any attempt to initiate

Behaviour

- Provide structure – clear expectations, direction and organisation
- Have classroom rules prominently displayed, containing no more than five clear, concrete and positive statements, i.e. 'do' rather than 'don't'
- Involve children in the formulation of rules and discuss and explain these frequently
- Ensure that the children closest to a child with ABI are good models of behaviour
- Establish a format for the start and finish of each lesson (e.g. have an activity that children can get on with as soon as they enter the classroom, have rules for leaving a classroom)
- Redirect behaviour to a different topic or activity that is more acceptable (e.g. gain the child's attention and change the conversation, or direct the child to an activity with which he is already familiar and competent, one that does not require further explanations)
- Keep level of stimulation low; be aware that bright lights, noise and a high activity level can create additional stress
- Establish clear routines – give notice of any changes

- Ensure child has clear timetable – time, location, activity, and teacher's name if appropriate – to cover the whole school day
- Provide choice and control whenever possible through acceptable choices towards an agreed goal (e.g. the order in which tasks are done, the materials used, etc.)
- Follow a directed task with one which allows choice
- Be consistent. It is important for boundaries to be clearly stated and the same limits set by all members of staff
- Establish close proximity when child is becoming anxious or excitable. Use the child's name and direct back to task with a statement that will serve as a prompt/reminder about what he is meant to be doing
- Monitor the child frequently – breakdown of self-control can happen quickly, resulting in behaviour difficulties. Be sensitive to changes in the child
- Establish a regular format for cueing the child when giving information (e.g. by using his name). Ensure eye contact
- Provide verbal and visual directions. Use gestures as well as words, written and/or pictorial information
- Ensure the child understands the task
- Model calm, controlled and predictable behaviour
- Provide clear statements that describe exactly what the desired behaviour is (e.g. 'Tom, please pick up your pen and continue to write your story about the invasion', rather than 'Tom, please behave yourself and get on')
- Be generous with approval of appropriate behaviour. Immediate feedback and reinforcement are important, so try to catch them behaving well and praise. State the specific behaviour that has been appropriate
- Expect variable performance and be prepared to modify expectations
- Help children to reflect on their own good behaviour (e.g. 'You sat quietly in the hall during assembly – that was great. What do you think about that?')

CHAPTER 11

Transitions

Returning to school is a series of transitions from the moment the student is injured until they graduate school and beyond, much like a chain that has a series of links tying itself together from beginning to end.

(Savage and Wolcott 1995)

Transitions imply change – change of class, change of year group, change of friends, change of school – which provoke alterations in expectations and responsibilities. It is important to remember that any change – any transition – will be potentially more difficult and demanding for the child with ABI than for other children and may provoke additional problems. However, the most common transition times when particular difficulties emerge are school transfers.

School transfers

Details relating to initial integration into school for a brain-injured preschooler or reintegration for an older child have been discussed in Chapter 5 and it is important to remember these same issues when the child faces transfer from one school to another or from one key stage to the next.

There are three main reasons for this.

Ability to cope with change

Children with cognitive difficulties following ABI frequently have problems coping with anything new, unexpected or different. They need consistent structure and routine. All children benefit from this, but those with ABI can become more anxious, disorientated and fatigued in novel situations than their typically developing peers. They may react with inappropriate behaviour – challenging or withdrawn – and their school work may deteriorate. It is, therefore, very important that such changes are well planned in advance and that gradual familiarisation with the new environment and routine is built into a plan for such a transition (this applies to any plan for change, not just the Year 9 Transition Plan for those with Statements of Special Educational Needs, although this is an ideal forum for good advance planning).

Impaired development and increasing demands

As children increase in age, they normally develop skills to be able to complete greater amounts of more complex work more independently and this is reflected in the demands of the curriculum and the school environment. However, as has been discussed, children with acquired brain injuries often show impairment of that developmental trajectory years after their injury. It is not unusual to see a child who seemed to have been doing well in primary education suddenly present with a range of difficulties following transfer to secondary school. This can also sometimes be seen after transfer to Key Stage 4. Therefore, it is very important to consider this *in advance*. It is important not to assume that the child will cope, but to give thought to the additional demands that will be made in order to ensure that appropriate support is put in place *before* difficulties become apparent. If necessary, levels of support can be reduced at a later stage.

Many other children find increasing demands difficult, for instance when transferring to a much larger and very different environment at Key Stage 3 and this has become a focus for additional support and guidance from both the DfES and LEAs, in addition to publications produced by other organisations, e.g. NASEN (the National Association for Special Educational Needs). These guidelines can also be helpful for those working with children with acquired brain injury, but must be used selectively or with adaptations to take into account knowledge of the child's acquired deficits. For example, maps and photographs of a new school environment are sometimes provided for young people to use as games prior to transfer to enable them to become familiar with the new school. The child with ABI may have any one of a number of cognitive or sensory difficulties that would make this approach inappropriate and, therefore, strategies need to be individually tailored to a child's needs.

Transfer of information

Even if appropriate information is provided for a school and good planning takes place during initial reintegration, information is often not passed on when a child transfers to a new teacher or a new setting. If support enables the child to do well, his underlying difficulties may be overlooked with the passage of time. Strategies can support the child to such an extent that it may seem that they are no longer necessary. This assumption should never be made unless there has been a controlled reduction or removal of any such supports – e.g. the use of a visual organiser – with a planned 'safety net'. Remember that, unfortunately, many of the problems caused by ABI cannot be 'cured', but it is possible to enable the child to learn to compensate for these. So, however well the child seems to be doing, it is always important to pass on all relevant information to any new placement or set of teachers. There may be a need for training or awareness raising for those who will subsequently be working with the child or young person. Continued assessment and monitoring remain essential. Partnership with parents is also vital and this is discussed in Chapter 12.

It is important that other professionals involved in planning transitions for the child or young person, such as Personal Advisers from Connexions, have an awareness of issues relating to ABI in order to advise appropriately.

Prior to any change:

- begin planning well in advance
- review relevant information, records and current provision
- consider the demands of the new setting or situation
- arrange preliminary visits for familiarisation
- involve parents or other family members in the process
- anticipate any increased difficulties or demands the child may face
- plan how to address these
- put in place any additional necessary resources or support in advance
- arrange any necessary staff training
- identify a key member of staff for liaison
- pass on all relevant information and documentation to that person
- check if the key person has any queries when he has read the information
- ensure there is an efficient system for disseminating relevant information to other staff members
- arrange a review soon after transfer to monitor provision and progress.

Post-16

Planning for post-16 provision must take into account the complex issues provoked by ABI and the factors listed above, whether this is in a school or college setting. Colleges of Further Education can increasingly provide significant special needs support, but staff need detailed information about learning and behaviour needs if they are to do so effectively.

Young people with ABI who have been aware of the difficulties that they have faced in school are all too often heard to say that everything will be different once they transfer to college. They are frequently unaware of the nature or level of their own difficulties and can assume that these are related to the school environment. A realisation that the problems are exactly the same, or probably more evident, once they begin a college course can provoke a major reduction of self-esteem and subsequent failure to complete courses. Unfortunately, too many of these young people begin one or multiple courses which they then fail to complete and then end up staying at home with very low self-esteem – or even with developing mental health problems – unable to initiate educational, employment or social activities.

Some young people do not want information about their difficulties to be passed on to college staff. Sometimes they will express a wish to 'move on' and to 'make a fresh start'. This must be carefully and sensitively handled. Hopefully, if they have been well supported in school, encouraged to see the benefit of appropriate provision and become aware of their needs and learning styles, then they will accept the need for transfer of information. However, if a young person remains resistant, then careful preparation work involving him and his parents will be necessary.

Some young people who have sustained severe brain injuries and who have a range of resultant difficulties are still able to pursue courses of higher education, but, once again, tutors must be made aware of their difficulties. Support for students with SEN and disabilities is also increasing at universities and provision can usually be put in place upon transfer of information. There may be the benefit of funds from a Disabled Student's Allowance to enable additional resources. It is important to ensure that information about the young person's difficulties is transferred to new tutors in subsequent years or modules within the course. Examination dispensation should be sought where appropriate.

CHAPTER 12

Working with families

My child is not what she was, nor will she be what she was to become. Neither am I. Neither is anyone else in my family.

(Parent, in Savage and Morales 1996)

In 1989, David Hall, Consultant Paediatrician, wrote: 'Although one may empathise with parents who have a head injured child, it may be that only those who have been through such trauma can really understand' (Hall 1989). It is important that we continue to recognise this and to understand its implications.

When the child first becomes ill or suffers an injury, the family's world can be turned upside down. It may not be clear initially if he will survive and parents find themselves in an alien medical world, where they can feel powerless to do what they most wish to do – care for their child – and have to leave him in the hands of strangers. As detailed in Chapter 2, stages of early recovery can be unpredictable and frightening. Parents and other family members can find themselves on a roller coaster of emotional reactions.

In addition to fear, powerlessness and anxiety, issues of guilt and blame are common. Occasionally, parents may be responsible for what has happened to their child, but more often than not the guilt is irrational, but this does not make it less disabling. Parents naturally want to care for and to protect their children and so often feel responsible if anything happens to them. It can be difficult for them to avoid the many, 'If only…' questions. They may, of course, blame someone else – a car driver, the adult or sibling who was looking after the child, etc.

Brothers and sisters also frequently feel guilt. This may be because they were present when their sibling was injured, or just because they are uninjured or have survived. It is not uncommon to find that siblings are secretly consumed by the idea that 'It should have been me'.

If the child remains in hospital for some time, additional strains are placed on the family. Often one parent will remain with the child in hospital and sometimes becomes totally involved in looking after him, to the exclusion of everything else. If there is a second parent, he or she may have to continue working – financial problems can add additional strain at this time – looking after other children and running the household. Huge strains can be placed upon the parents' relationship. If the injured child has a single parent, extended family members may be involved.

Parents frequently say that they cannot wait for their child to be discharged from hospital and think that this will mark a turning point towards full recovery. Often children do show a significant spurt in progress when they first return home and this encourages parents to hope for a full recovery.

> After hovering near death in a comatose state, this experience of reemergence was a powerful one. ...parents felt they had very strong emotional evidence to prove the worthiness of their undying hope. ...Some parents did not understand that their child was forever changed until long after the accident.
>
> (Singer and Nixon 1996)

Sometimes, although parents do recognise many of the difficulties faced by their child and the differences in him, the full extent of these is only something that they come to realise or to accept over a long time. They have seen the remarkable progress that he has made from the time of his acute illness or injury. Why should they not believe that this will continue? In order to cope, they may only be able to accept or to understand a certain amount at any one time. Savage and Morales (1996) quote a parent who overhead a nurse saying that he was in 'denial'. He was well aware that he was in 'survival' rather than denial! It can be very easy for others to be judgemental regarding parents' reactions.

We all have different coping strategies. Some parents put huge amounts of energy into information gathering; some seek alternative therapies or treatments; some seek support from the Church or from voluntary organisations; some refer to their child's difficulties frequently, others refuse to speak about them.

Whether or not they understand the full extent or impact of the child's difficulties, it is nevertheless parents and other family members who do see changes. Frequently these are changes to the child's personality and ability. They may appear subtle, or even non-existent to others, but to the family, this person is different. Parents have lost a child that they knew. It is not surprising, therefore, that the reactions that this provokes are often compared with those seen when someone is bereaved. However, there are some crucial differences:

> The unique tragedy of brain injury, as compared to other terrible illnesses or accidents, is the loss of the person and their replacement by someone different. This new person is not totally different but is a pale shadow of the former self, a constant reminder of the lost child. Often it is the person's less desirable characteristics which are prominent. This situation is unlike the death of a child. The parents have no chance to finally accept and adjust; each day they have to deal with their grief again.
>
> (Hall 1989)

Research has confirmed the level of stress and anxiety suffered by parents of a child with ABI on an ongoing basis (Hawley *et al.* 2003).

It is important not to ignore the continuing difficulties faced by siblings. A younger brother or sister may have to take on a more mature role – to suddenly 'grow up' much more quickly and look after an older brother. If the injured child's behaviour is unusual or inappropriate this may be a cause of major embarrassment to his brothers and sisters. They may not want to be seen with him or to bring their friends home. They may feel unwanted or neglected, as their parents seem to be focusing on their injured brother. If tensions are apparent within their parents' relationship, children may blame their injured sibling. Subsequent unhappiness, anxiety, depression or behavioural difficulties exhibited by their other children can, in turn, cause further anxiety for the parents.

As the child so often seems to have made a good recovery, when he returns to school it can be the case that few problems are envisaged. Schools are frequently very positive in relation to the child's prospects and to their ability to address any apparent difficulties. Parents are frequently delighted that he is able to return to school and that the teachers are so encouraging.

However, many parents say that they then begin to realise that their child is facing difficulties and that these are not being recognised, but their concerns may be dismissed by school staff. The most frequent comment heard from these parents regarding their child's school is, 'They just don't seem to understand!' Some parents give up trying to tell staff about their concerns at this stage, whereas others become increasingly vociferous and sometimes angry. School staff may then consider them to be over-anxious or awkward.

Conversely, schools sometimes report that parents expect too much of their child and refuse to accept his learning difficulties. This must be understood in the light of their previous aspirations based on his potential at that time and the difficulties inherent in accepting any changes to this.

Another issue that frequently causes disagreement or misunderstanding between parents and schools is the effect of events or incidents reported by the child. As a result of the cognitive difficulties frequently faced by these children, their ability to accurately interpret situations or other people's actions may be impaired. It is relatively common for these children to go home and report, for instance, bullying by other children or unfair treatment by staff. There are, of course, times when this may be accurate, but there are also many where this is not the case but is undoubtedly the child's perception of events. Understandably, the parent often believes the child's version of events and, therefore, understanding and good communication is required to avoid conflicts or resentment.

It is of crucial importance that schools work with parents to meet the needs of a child. In order to do this effectively for a child with ABI, school staff must have an understanding of the parents' situation and of the child's difficulties. There are some basic guidelines, which are important to keep in mind:

- Recognise the nature and extent of the trauma with which the family as a whole has had to cope and is still coping
- Always listen to what parents have to say. Never dismiss their opinions. They know their child better than anyone else
- Never be judgemental of parents. Do not take criticism personally
- Recognise why they might find it hard to accept their child's limitations
- Accept and consider their descriptions of the difficulties the child is encountering
- Find out about the possible effects of acquired brain injury
- Keep communicating with the child's parents. Ask for their opinion – remember that they are partners in their child's education
- Ask parents what strategies they find useful at home to address the child's problems
- Be prepared to be flexible
- Do not make assumptions.

It is interesting to note that some examples of schools where parents and staff have been seen to work closely together, ensuring that the child's needs have been well met, are those where school staff have been very aware of or have witnessed the child's injury. This may be because the child was involved in a road traffic accident outside the school. Staff may have seen this happen; may have comforted other children and parents; may have seen paramedics working on the child and may have watched an ambulance or air ambulance arrive. When school staff have also been involved in some way in that initial trauma, they remain more conscious of the effects of this on the family. However, when a child enters a class or school looking well, perhaps years after his injury, members of staff do not have the benefit of that knowledge or memory. It is important that they take into account what the family has experienced.

Some of the best examples of educational provision designed to meet the needs of children with ABI have been planned in conjunction and co-operation with parents and with a flexible basis. When teachers do listen to parents, without preconceived ideas, they can often find ways of incorporating their ideas and suggestions to excellent effect. This is true partnership.

> Every step of the way for the past six and a half years, my wife and I have struggled to deal with people from a variety of professions who are ignorant of the complexities of acquired brain injury. From lawyers to medics to educationalists we have discovered that there is a serious lack of both knowledge and understanding. ...Currently the child is expected to access their learning from within one of a small selection of boxes. This system is fundamentally flawed because it fails to recognise the specific individual requirements of the child. ...A brain-injured child need not always become a disabled adult, dependent upon others for their very existence, but they do need to receive an education to enable them to reach their full potential. (Parent of a child with ABI)

CHAPTER 13

Mild traumatic brain injury

No head injury is too severe to despair of nor too trivial to ignore.

(Translation from Hippocrates, fourth century BC)

There are definitions of mild brain injury, which relate to medical measurements, the most commonly used being the Glasgow Coma Scale (Teasdale and Jennet 1974). This assesses a person's level of responsiveness. A child with a mild injury may not lose consciousness – or if he does it will not be for a significant length of time – but will suffer a concussion (see types below). He may not be admitted to hospital or may only be kept there for overnight observation.

In the past, it was generally thought that, whereas moderate or severe acquired brain injuries frequently provoke lasting effects relating to a child's cognitive or social functioning, mild injuries were unlikely to cause such difficulties. This is important, because the largest proportion of such injuries sustained by children can be classified as mild and many children who sustain minor concussions may never even be referred to a doctor.

However, there is increasing concern that even mild injuries can cause long-lasting effects. Equally, some children with severe injuries show a much fuller recovery of functions than do others. It has also been of concern to those who study the effects of trauma to the brain that minor concussion has often been discounted by many as trivial, without consideration of possible effects.

Review of research shows that there continues to be no universally accepted definition of what constitutes a mild brain injury. Different researchers have used differing criteria in their studies, which does not facilitate clear understanding of the issues. This partly reflects the fact that assessment of young children who have sustained such injuries can be difficult. Standard assessment of levels of consciousness using accepted scales can be problematic in young children, as their responses cannot be measured in the same way as those of an older child or adult. It may be difficult to establish if a young child lost consciousness and for how long.

It could, therefore, be the case that some children have actually suffered a more or less serious injury than has been diagnosed, which could account, to some extent, for differences in outcome.

There is considerable interest in research to establish if some people are more susceptible to the effects of acquired brain injury than others.

Research indicates that children who are classed as having suffered a mild acquired brain injury frequently do less well on psychometric assessments in the short term (e.g. Mathias *et al.* 2004). Some controversy relates to the possible lasting effects of these difficulties. Some researchers claim evidence of ongoing difficulties, for instance with attention or with behaviour, following a mild brain injury. However, others claim that these are more likely to be linked to pre-existing difficulties – children with attentional or behavioural problems are more likely to sustain such injuries – and to ongoing social or environmental factors.

Some young people who have sustained a mild brain injury have shown decreased academic achievement and increased levels of anxiety for much longer than would be expected. It is noticeable that, when this occurs, the injuries have often been sustained at a crucial time during the young person's education, e.g. just prior to GCSE examinations. They have returned to school immediately with no specific advice having been given to them or to their families. It is likely that certain key skills, such as those relating to attention, speed of processing, or memory will have decreased initially. It is possible that the anxiety provoked by this, particularly at a time of relatively high academic demands, has caused an exacerbation and continuation of the difficulties. Research supports the conclusions that cognitive challenges and insufficient provision of information can both increase and extend the symptoms of mild traumatic brain injury (Hanna-Pladdy *et al.* 2001, Ponsford *et al.* 2001). Interestingly, in Canada where there is a system whereby victims of road traffic accidents receive compensation from a central organisation, a checklist is used to identify children who are at risk from longer-term effects of mild brain injury. One factor on the list is: 'lack of social and educational support, high social and educational expectations' (Bourque 2003). This also indicates an appreciation that lack of appropriate social or educational support or understanding provokes longer-term difficulties for children with mild TBI.

The clear indications from all this are that advice should be given to young people following such an injury and that school staff should be aware, supportive and understanding.

Recent studies relate to concussions on the sports field. Researchers in the US recruited college football players for comprehensive studies (McCrea *et al.* 2003). It was predicted that a percentage of these young men would suffer concussive injuries while engaged in their sport. Initial cognitive assessments were conducted on all the subjects in order that baselines were established. Whenever one of the footballers sustained a concussive injury, they were reassessed immediately and then at regular intervals. This showed reduced performance initially, despite the fact that the teenagers generally insisted that they felt fine, with re-establishment of normal levels of functioning usually within approximately one week.

This indicates that there is likely to be a reduction in academic ability for a short time following even a brief concussion and schools should be aware of this. Following a mild TBI, young people may show:

- reduced levels of concentration
- reduced memory skills
- reduced speeds of processing information
- reduced academic attainment
- frustration or anxiety relating to the above
- irritability.

All of the above will normally be short-lived, but may persist depending on the child's circumstances and could lead to further anxiety and/or depression.

Hospitals may give information cards to the parents of children attending with mild TBI. These include information about signs to look out for following such an injury and it is important to be vigilant about this. If school staff notice any changes following such an injury (e.g. confusion, dizziness, vomiting, sleepiness) the child's parents should be informed and medical attention sought.

Some research also indicates that, during the period of recovery from concussion, our brains are much more vulnerable to the effects of subsequent injury. If a young person who has had one blow to the head then experiences another, in rare cases the effects could be far more severe, or even fatal (Cantu 1998). This effect has been termed 'Second Impact Syndrome'. It is generally accepted to be very important that young people who sustain a concussion must not be allowed to engage in activities that carry the risk of a second such injury until they have fully recovered. This means that, for instance, rugby and soccer players who sustain such injuries in schools should not be allowed straight back on the pitch.

The American Academy of Neurology makes recommendations regarding the length of time **with no symptoms** that should elapse before someone is allowed to return to the sports field following concussion. It is important that the absence of symptoms is apparent *while exercising* as well as at rest. The Academy defines three grades of concussion:

Grade 1 – the child is conscious, but confused for anything up to 15 minutes.

Grade 2 – the same as Grade 1, except that the child also has some loss of memory for what happened and symptoms last longer than 15 minutes.

Grade 3 – loss of consciousness for any length of time, however brief.

The table below shows the Academy's recommended times before returning to sport for each grade of concussion:

Severity of concussion	Time before returning to sport
Grade 1	15 minutes or less
Several at Grade 1	1 week
Grade 2	1 week
Several at Grade 2	2 weeks
Grade 3	
Unconscious for seconds	1 week
Unconscious for minutes	2 weeks
Several at Grade 3	1 month or longer, based on medical advice

Useful organisations and resources

All of the websites below were operational at the time of going to press. However, the precise addresses of websites can be unreliable due to pages being updated, reorganised, or even disappearing altogether. If this happens, try typing key words into a search engine.

Education

Acquire (formerly HIRE, Head Injury Re-Education) provides information regarding the education of children, young people and adults with ABI. Manor House Farm, Wendlebury, Bicester, Oxon, OX25 2PW Tel: 01869 324339 www.acquire.org.uk

Advisory Centre for Education (ACE) is an independent advice centre for parents covering a range of issues, e.g. exclusion, bullying, special educational needs. A Special Education handbook gives practical advice for parents about a range of SEN issues. General Advice line: 0808 800 5793 Exclusion information line: 020 7704 9822 www.ace-ed.org.uk

Becta (British Educational Communications and Technology Agency) is a government agency for ICT education www.becta.org.uk

Connexions is a government support service for 13 to 19-year-olds, providing information on courses, careers, personal development, etc. www.connexions.gov.uk

Department for Education and Skills (DfES) provides a number of useful resources: special needs information can be found at www.dfes.gov.uk/sen; a catalogue of resources to support individual learning needs at http://inclusion.ngfl.gov.uk; a list of all Local Education Authorities and links to other education sites at www.dfes.gov.uk/leagateway; a parents' website at www.dfes.gov.uk/parents and a copy of the document *Access to Education for Children and Young People with Medical Needs* and related information at www.dfes.gov.uk/sickchildren

Enchanted Learning provides easy to read information about the brain and a few suggested classroom activities www.enchantedlearning.com

Independent Panel for Special Education Advice (IPSEA) provides help, support and information for parents of children with special educational needs. Freephone: 0800 0184016 www.ipsea.org.uk

Joint Council for Qualifications publishes a document of regulations and guidance relating to examination candidates with particular requirements, giving details of arrangements and allowances made each year for candidates who require something different from the standard arrangements for assessment, e.g. extra time, amanuensis, etc. www.jcq.org.uk

Learning and Skills Council is responsible for funding and planning education and training for over-16s. Also runs an 'Entry to Employment' scheme for 16 to 18-year-olds who are not currently in education, training or employment to help them with the transition into learning and jobs www.lsc.gov.uk

National Parent Partnership Network provides information, support and advice for parents of children with special educational needs. Tel: 0207 843 600 www.parentpartnership.org.uk

National Society for Special Educational Needs promotes training and development, and produces journals and policy documents and other publications on a range of special educational issues www.nasen.org.uk

Network 81 1–7 Woodfield Terrace, Stansted, Essex, CM24 8AJ. Helpline: 0870 770 3306. Provides information and advice for parents of children with special educational needs, including publications, advice on communicating with schools and education authorities, newsletter, 'befrienders' who can support parents at meetings and during the assessment process http://network81.co.uk

Neuroscience for Kids is a web-base dedicated to providing information for children, students and teachers who want to learn more about the brain and spinal cord. It includes a range of activities such as games, model making etc. http://faculty.washington.edu/chudler/neurok.html

notschool.net is a virtual community that aims to give young people who are not engaged with the more traditional education systems, opportunity to develop self-esteem www.notschool.net

The Parent Centre offers support, information and advice about children's learning and the education system in England and Wales www.parentcentre.gov.uk

Parents for Inclusion is a national charity run by parents for parents. Helpline: 0800 652 3145 www.parentsforinclusion.org

Parents Online provides information for parents about primary school education www.parents.org.uk

Qualifications and Curriculum Authority (QCA) maintains and develops school curriculum and associated assessments www.qca.org.uk. A further site with guidance for school staff who work with children with learning difficulties is at www.nc.uk.net/id

Rathbone Special Education Advice Line. Tel: 0800 917 6790 (or 0800 085 4528 for Urdu, Punjabi, Gujarati, Bengali and Hindi speakers) www.rathbonetraining.co.uk

Scientific Learning create computer-based programs for specific learning difficulties www.scilearn.com

Skill National Bureau for Students with Disabilities in post-16 education. Chapter House, 18–20 Crucifix Lane, London, SE1 3JW Freephone helpline: 0800 328 5050 www.skill.org.uk

Special Educational Needs & Disability Tribunal publish a document (2002) *Special Educational Needs: How to Appeal.* Also a video *Right to be Heard* available from Windsor House, 50 Victoria St, London, SW1H 0NW Tel 020 7925 6925 www.sendist.gov.uk

Teachernet provides a wide range of information for teachers with links to numerous sites www.teachernet.gov.uk

Health

Adders provides information for raising awareness about ADD and ADHD, together with practical advice www.adders.org

Irish Sensory Integration Association 60 Bawnmore Road, Belfast, BT9 6LB Northern Ireland

Kids Health is a jargon-free health information site that has separate areas of age-appropriate content for children, teenagers and parents www.kidshealth.org

Sensory Integration Network www.sinetwork.org

Young Minds is a children's mental health charity which offers a range of information and materials on mental health issues www.youngminds.org.uk

Counselling

The British Association for Counselling and Psychotherapy (BACP) is the professional body in the UK that sets and monitors practice and standards in counselling and psychotherapy www.bacp.co.uk

Counselling in Education (CIE) is the expert practitioner group within BACP responsible for providing advice, guidance and consultation to anyone who is involved in enabling children and young people to have access to counselling. A *Guidance Booklet on Counselling in Schools* is available on the website. www.cie.uk.com

Disability rights

Disability Rights Commission (DRC) provides advice and information for parents. It has produced a Code of Practice for schools and parents, outlining rights and equality of access, and a Code of Practice for providers of post-16 education www.drc-gb.org

Inclusive Solutions provides information about techniques to consider for group work that promotes social/emotional skills www.inclusive-solutions.com

General behaviour difficulties

Framework for Intervention is the name given to a problem-solving approach designed by Birmingham education department for the entire school age range, with an emphasis on developing and managing the best possible behavioural environment. Publications and training courses provide detailed recommendations www.frameworkforintervention.com

Guidance on Physical Intervention is provided in the DfES and Department of Health (DoH) (2002) joint guidance document (LEA/0242/2002) *Use of Restrictive Physical Interventions for Staff Working with Children and Adults who Display Extreme Behaviour in Association with Learning Difficulties and/or Autistic Spectrum Disorders.* The guidance is aimed particularly at special schools catering for pupils with severe behavioural difficulties associated with learning and/or autistic spectrum disorders.

Sexual behaviour

DfES (2001) leaflet on Sex and Relationship Education available from DfES publications. Tel: 0845 602 2260, quote ref. DfES 0706/2001

The Family Planning Association offers a range of pamphlets, books, resource packs and videos on sexual matters. There are two books designed for young people with learning difficulties: 'Talking about…Growing Up' and 'Talking about…Sex and Relationships' www.fpa.org.uk

The National Children's Bureau provides fact sheets on sex education and approaches to teaching it. The Sex Education Forum at the National Children's Bureau offers a wealth of information about sex and relationships for teachers, carers and parents, including information sheets and a CD-Rom interactive resource www.ncb.org.uk/resources

Other charities relevant to ABI

AFASIC (Information and training to support young people with speech, language and communication impairments.) 2nd Floor, 50–52 Great Sutton St, London EC1V 0DJ Helpline: 08453 555577 www.afasic.org.uk

Association for Spina Bifida and Hydrocephalus (ASBAH) 42 Park Road, Peterborough PE1 2UQ Tel: 01733 555988 www.asbah.org

Ataxia UK 10 Winchester House, Kennington Park, Cranmer Road, London SW9 6EJ Tel: 020 7582 1444 Helpline: 020 7820 3900 www.ataxia.org.uk

Brain and Spine Foundation 7 Winchester House, Kennington Park, Cranmer Road, London SW9 6EJ Helpline: 0808 808 1000 www.brainandspine.org.uk

Brain and Spine Injury Charity (BASIC) The Neurocare Centre, 554 Eccles New Road, Salford M5 1AL Tel: 0161 707 6441 www.basiccharity.org.uk

Child Brain Injury Trust The Radcliffe Infirmary, Woodstock Road, Oxford OX2 6HE Tel: 01865 552 467 Helpline: 0845 601 4939 www.cbituk.org

Children's Hemiplegia and Stroke Association (US based) www.hemikids.org

Contact-a-Family 209–211 City Road, London EC1V 1JN Tel: 020 7608 8700 Helpline: 0808 808 3555 www.cafamily.org.uk

Different Strokes ('Charity set up by younger stroke survivors to support younger stroke survivors') 9 Canon Harnett Court, Wolverton Mill, Milton Keynes MK12 5NF Tel: 0845 130 7172 www.differentstrokes.co.uk

Epilepsy Action (formerly British Epilepsy Association) New Anstey House, Gate Way Drive, Yeadon, Leeds LS19 7XY Helpline: 0808 800 5050 www.epilepsy.org.uk

Headway, the brain injury association 4 King Edward Court, King Edward Street, Nottingham NG1 1EW Tel: 0115 924 0800 Helpline: 0808 800 2244 www.headway.org.uk

Hemihelp (Support and information about young people with hemiplegia) Unit 1, Wellington Works, Wellington Road, London SW19 8EQ Tel: 0845 120 3713 Helpline: 0845 123 2372 www.hemihelp.org.uk

National Meningitis Trust Fern House, Bath Road, Stroud, Gloucestershire GL5 3TJ Tel: 01453 76000 Helpline: 0845 6000 800 www.meningitis-trust.org.uk

The National Society for Epilepsy (NSE) Chesham Lane, Chalfont St Peter, Buckinghamshire SL9 0RJ Tel: 01494 601300 Helpline: 01494 601400 www.epilepsynse.org.uk

National Tremor Foundation Harold Wood Hospital (DSC), Gubbins Lane, Romford, Essex RM3 0BE Freephone: 0800 328 8046 www.tremor.org.uk

The Encephalitis Society 7b Saville Street, Malton, North Yorkshire YO17 7LL Tel: 01653 699599 www.encephalitis.info

The Stroke Association Stroke House, 240 City Road, London EC1V 2PR Helpline: 0845 30 33 100 www.stroke.org.uk

Safety and injury prevention

Bicycle Helmet Initiative Trust 1st floor, 43–45 Milford Road, Reading, Berkshire RG1 8LG Tel: 0118 9583585. Campaigns for greater use of bicycle helmets and offers information on usage of helmets. For price list, order forms and instructions on the wearing of helmets, visit www.bhit.org

Child Accident Prevention Trust (CAPT) 4th Floor, 18–20 Farringdon Lane, London EC1R 3HA Tel: 020 7608 3828 www.capt.org.uk

National Injury Prevention Foundation Site (US based) provides information on educating children about activities which place them at risk of a brain or spinal cord injury www.thinkfirst.org

Other publications

Transitions

From Key Stage 2 to Key Stage 3: Smoothing the Transfer for Pupils With Learning Difficulties, Dorothy Smith, NASEN, 2000.

Epilepsy

Epilepsy – a Teacher's Guide
Epilepsy and Higher Education } (Both available online from Epilepsy Action)

Your Child's Epilepsy: A Parent's Guide, R. Appleton, B. Chappell and M. Beirne, Class Publishing, 1997 (Available through National Society for Epilepsy)

Epilepsy: A Practical Guide (Resource Materials for Teachers), M. Johnson and G. Parkinson, David Fulton Publishers, 2002

Sensory integration

Sensory Integration and the Child, A. Jean Ayres, Western Psychological Society, 2001 (Recommended for parents)

Sensory Integration Theory and Practice, Second Edition, A. G. Fisher, E. A. Murray, A. C. Bundy, F. A. Davis Company, 2002 (Recommended for professionals)

(Both available from Sensory Integration International at www.sensoryint.com)

For siblings of children with ABI

Sam and the Green Velvet Monkey (a storybook for young children)
You're Not the Only One (for teenagers)
(Both CBIT publications)

For children with ABI

Elvin the Elephant Who Forgets, H. Snyder and S. Beebe (for young children)
(Available from Acquire)

For parents of children with ABI

Choosing a School for Your Child With Acquired Brain Injury, S. Walker and B. Wicks

A range of booklets and Tip Cards relating to issues following ABI in childhood (for parents and teachers)

(Available from Acquire)

Must Try Harder (A booklet and video about the educational needs of children with ABI for parents to share with teachers)

(Available from Acquire or CBIT)

Headstrong – all about brain tumors (Resources to help children understand their illness and cope with treatment). www.headstrongkids.org.uk. Brain and Spine Foundation

Learning from the Experts (Series of information leaflets written by young people with ABI) CBIT

Glossary

Amnesia: lack of memory about events occurring during a particular period of time

Ankle foot orthosis (AFO): a moulded brace that stabilises the ankle joint

Anoxia: lack of oxygen to the brain

Anti-convulsants: medication to prevent or reduce seizures

Ataxia: movements characterised by incoordination, tremor or both and caused by damage to the brain. Ataxia can affect fine motor skills, gross motor skills and speech

Axons: the usually long and straight part of a neuron or nerve cell that conducts impulses (messages) away from the cell body to another neuron

Bilateral: referring to both sides of the body

Brainstem: the lower extension of the brain where it connects to the spinal cord. Survival (breathing, heart rate) and arousal (being awake and alert) functions are located in the brainstem

Central nervous system (CNS): the brain and spinal cord

Cerebellum: part of the brain located at the back, below the cortex, that relates particularly to movement (damage to this area can provoke ataxia)

Cerebral cortex: the outer part of the brain, made up of two hemispheres, each with four lobes (frontal, temporal, parietal, occipital)

Cerebrospinal fluid (CSF): a colourless fluid that is produced in the brain and fills the space in the brain called the ventricles. It circulates around the brain and spinal cord

Closed head/brain injury: one type of traumatic brain injury. In this type of injury, the skull is not penetrated. It is the most common type of injury and often occurs from road traffic accidents, falls, or shaking in babies

Cognition: the processes involved in thinking, learning, knowing and problem solving

Coma: a state of unconsciousness following injury to the brain from which the person cannot be roused, characterised by lack of voluntary eye opening, response to simple commands or comprehensible speech

Computerised tomography (CT) or **computerised axial tomography (CAT):** scans involving a series of images taken at different levels of the brain (or other parts of the body)

Concussion: an alteration of consciousness caused by an injury to the brain (usually a blow to the head)

Contrecoup: the word coup in French means strike or blow. Contrecoup refers to an injury at the opposite side of the brain to the original impact, when the brain rebounds within the skull

Contusion: bruise

Corpus callosum: a band of fibres that connects the two hemispheres of the brain and enables rapid communication between them

Cyst: an abnormal sac or cavity filled with liquid or semi-solid matter

Dendrites: 'branches' extending from neurons or nerve cells that carry incoming signals into the cell

Diffuse axonal injury: widespread injury to the brain caused by shearing (tearing) of axons (see above) as a result of acceleration/deceleration injuries, such as in a road traffic accident

Diplopia: seeing two images of a single object (double vision)

Disinhibition: inability to suppress impulsive speech or actions

Dysarthria: a motor speech disorder caused by weakness, slowness or incoordination of the muscles involved in speech. The severity can range from no ability to produce intelligible speech to a mild articulation difficulty

Dysphasia: impaired ability to communicate with and/or to understand language

Dyspraxia: impaired ability to plan and execute co-ordinated or sequenced movements

Echolalia: repetition of words or speech sounds without comprehension or meaning as communication

EEG (electroencephalogram): the trace of a recording of electrical activity in different parts of the brain

Emotional lability: sudden changes or extreme reactions of emotional state

Encephalopathy: any of various diseases that affect the functioning of the brain

Epilepsy: a group of disorders of brain function, due to uncoordinated electrical activity, that are characterised by recurrent attacks with sudden onset

Executive functions: include the ability to set goals, plan and strategically problem solve, initiate actions, inhibit inappropriate responses and monitor or control behaviour. The frontal lobes are mainly responsible for executive functions, but other areas are also involved

Fine motor skills: small physical actions such as those made by the hands, fingers and toes

Focal brain injury: an injury solely to a specific area of the brain (rare in traumatic brain injury)

Frontal lobes: the part of the brain at the front (left and right). This area of the brain plays a role in controlling emotions, motivation, social skills, expressive language, inhibition of impulses, planning, organising, problem solving, and higher level cognitive (or executive) skills

Gait: walking pattern

Glasgow Coma Scale (GCS): a frequently used scale to help towards assessing the severity of a brain injury, based on three components of consciousness: eye opening, verbal response and motor movement. A mild brain injury is usually thought to correspond to a score of 13–15, a moderate injury to a score of 9–12, and a severe injury to a score of 3–8. The lowest possible score for a live person is 3

Glial cells: cells in the brain that are not neurons (nerve cells). These represent about 90 per cent of the total and their exact function is unknown, but the word glial means glue and they do hold the structure together

Gross motor skills: actions performed by large muscle groups (i.e. major body movements)

Haematoma: a collection of blood within tissue that then clots

Haemorrhage: the escape of blood from a ruptured blood vessel

Hemianopia: an inability to see within one half of the visual field

Hemiparesis: a weakness (affecting movement or use of limbs) on one side of the body

Hemiplegia: a degree of paralysis of limbs on one side of the body

Hemisphere: one half of the brain – either left or right

Hydrocephalus: an abnormal increase in the amount of cerebrospinal fluid in the ventricles of the brain, causing increased intracranial pressure

Hypoxia: insufficient oxygen supply to tissues of the body

Intracranial pressure: the pressure level within the skull, altered by swelling of tissue or increase in amount of cerebrospinal fluid

Ischaemia: an inadequate flow of blood to a part of the body, caused by constriction or blockage of the blood vessels supplying it

Limbic system: area at the upper end of the brainstem that contains structures relating, among other things, to emotion and memory

Magnetic resonance imaging (MRI): a computer imaging technique that produces more detailed scans to generate images of internal structure of the brain

Meninges: three protective layers covering the brain and spinal cord

Metacognition: insight into strengths and weaknesses with regard to learning (cognition) – knowing how you learn

Motor control: Fine – co-ordination of muscles to make intricate movements, particularly involving the hands; **Gross** – co-ordination of muscles to make large body movements

Neonatal: the time from birth up to six weeks old

Neurologist: a doctor who specialises in the nervous system

Neuron: a nerve cell within the brain

Neuropsychologist: a psychologist who specialises in the cognitive and behavioural changes related to brain abnormalities. A paediatric neuropsychologist specialises in the problems of children with brain disorders

Occipital lobe: the posterior section of each hemisphere of the brain, including areas responsible for interpretation of visual images

Oedema: excess build-up of fluid in body tissue, often causing swelling

Open head/brain injury: a type of brain injury where the skull is penetrated and the underlying brain exposed

Parietal lobe: the upper middle part of each side of the brain, behind the frontal lobes. Responsible, for instance, for visuo-spatial skills (right hemisphere) and some language functions (usually left hemisphere)

Perseveration: inappropriate repetition of actions, thoughts or speech

Post-traumatic amnesia (PTA): a time following a brain injury when a person does not have reliable continuous memory for day-to-day events. This is a good indicator of severity of injury, but can be difficult to assess in young children

Premorbid: prior to onset of illness or injury

Proprioception: awareness of the position of parts of the body without visual feedback (e.g. knowing where your hand is and being able to touch it with the other without looking)

Psychometric assessments: standardised tests to assess cognitive functioning

Quadriparesis: weakness of all four limbs

Quadriplegia: a degree of paralysis of all four limbs (sometimes termed tetraplegia)

Rancho Los Amigos Scale of Cognitive Functions: a measure of the stages of recovery following a brain injury

Reinforcement: any consequence that increases the likelihood of the occurrence of a particular behaviour

Retrograde amnesia: an inability to remember information from a specific length of time prior to a brain injury (e.g. minutes to months)

Shunt: in this context, a valve and tube surgically inserted to drain excess cerebrospinal fluid from the brain to the chest or abdominal cavity

Spasticity: causes an involuntary increase in muscle tone when limbs are moved, provoking resistance. Caused by brain or spinal cord damage

Temporal lobe: the lower middle part of each side of the brain. Thought to be involved in memory function, among other things

Tracheostomy: a temporary surgical opening at the throat to assist breathing

Traumatic brain injury (TBI): an acquired brain injury caused by an external physical force – in an accident (or as a non-accidental injury)

Tremor: involuntary quivering movements

Unilateral: relating to only one side of the body

Unilateral neglect: lack of awareness either of one side of a person's own body, of anything external to one side of the body, or of both

Ventilator: a machine that maintains a flow of air into and out of the lungs when someone is unable to breathe normally

Ventricles: four cavities within the brain that are filled with cerebrospinal fluid

References

Anderson, P. (2002) 'Assessment and development of executive function during childhood', *Child Neuropsychology*, 8(2), 71–82.

Anderson,V., Northam, E., Hendy, J. and Wrennall, J. (2001) *Developmental Neuropsychology – A Clinical Approach.* Hove, East Sussex: Psychology Press.

Anderson, V. and Pentland, L. (1998) 'Residual attention deficits following childhood head injury', *Neuropsychological Rehabilitation*, 8(3), 283–300.

Appleton, R. and Baldwin, T. (1998) *Management of Brain Injured Children.* Oxford: Oxford University Press.

Beardmore, S., Tate, R. and Liddle, B. (1999) 'Does information and feedback improve children's knowledge and awareness of deficits after traumatic brain injury?', *Neuropsychological Rehabilitation*, 9(1), 45–62.

Birnbaum, R. and Deutsch, R. (1996) 'The use of dynamic assessment and its relationship to the Code of Practice: working across boundaries', *Educational & Child Psychology*, 13(3), 14–24.

Blosser, J. L. and DePompei, R. (1994) 'Creating an effective classroom environment', in Savage, R. C. and Wolcott, G. F. (eds) *Educational Dimensions of Acquired Brain Injury.* Austin, TX: Pro-Ed, pp. 413–51.

Blosser, R. and DePompei, R. (2003) *Pediatric Traumatic Brain Injury – Proactive Intervention*, 2nd edn. Delmar: Thompson Learning.

Bourque, C. (2003) *A Screening and Early Intervention Procedure for Mild Brain Injury Children and Adolescents Who are at Risk of Developing Persistent Symptoms: a Preventive Approach.* Poster presentation at 5th World Congress on Brain Injury, Stockholm, Sweden.

Bryant, R. and Harvey, A. (1998) 'Traumatic memories and pseudomemories in post traumatic stress disorder', *Applied Cognitive Psychology*, 12, 81–88.

Camis, J. (2001) *My Life and Me.* London: British Association for Adoption and Fostering.

Cantu, R. C. (1998) 'Second-impact syndrome', *Clinics in Sports Medicine*, 17, 37–44.

Carter, R. (1998) *Mapping the Mind.* London: Phoenix.

Clark, E. (1997) 'Children and adolescents with traumatic brain injury: reintegration challenges in educational settings', in Bigler, E., Clark, E. and Farmer, J. (eds) *Childhood Traumatic Brain Injury,* Austin, TX: Pro-Ed, pp. 191–211.

Connor, M. (1997) 'Parental motivation for specialist or mainstream placement', *Support for Learning,* 12(3), 104–10.

Crouchman, M. (1998) 'Recovery, rehabilitation and the neuropsychological sequelae of head injury', in Ward Platt, M. and Little, R. (eds) *Injury in the Young.* Cambridge: Cambridge University Press, pp. 263–99.

Deaton, A. (1994) 'Changing the behaviors of students with acquired brain injuries', in Savage, R. C. and Wolcott, G. F. (eds) *Educational Dimensions of Acquired Brain Injury,* Austin, TX: Pro-Ed, pp. 257–76.

Department for Education and Skills (DfES) (2001a) *Access to Education for Children and Young People with Medical Needs,* ref: 0732/2001. London: DfES.

Department for Education and Skills (DfES) (2001b) *Special Educational Needs Code of Practice.* London: DfES.

Department for Education and Skills (DfES) (2001c) SEN Toolkit *Section 4: Enabling Pupil Participation,* ref. 558/2001. London: DfES.

Department for Education and Skills (DfES) (2003) *National Agreement on School Workforce Reforms.* London: DfES.

DePompei, R. and Blosser, J. (1994) 'The family as collaborator for effective school reintegration', in Savage, R. C. and Wolcott, G. F. (eds) *Educational Dimensions of Acquired Brain Injury.* Austin, TX: Pro-Ed, pp. 489–506.

Deutsch, R. and Reynolds, Y. (2000) 'The use of dynamic assessment by educational psychologists in the UK', *Educational Psychology in Practice,* 16(3), pp. 311–31.

Feeney, J. and Ylvisaker, M. (1997) 'A positive, communication-based approach to challenging behaviour after ABI', in Glang, A., Singer, G. *et al.* (eds) *Students with Acquired Brain Injury – The School's Response,* Baltimore, MD: Paul H. Brookes, pp. 229–54.

Fenwick, T. and Anderson, V. (1999) 'Impairments of attention following traumatic brain injury', *Child Neuropsychology,* 5(4), 213–23.

Fletcher, J., Ewing-Cobbs, L., Francis, D. and Levin, H. (1995) 'Variability in outcomes after traumatic brain injury in children: a developmental perspective', in Broman, S. H. and Michel, M. E. (eds) *Traumatic Head Injury in Children.* Oxford: Oxford University Press, pp. 3–21.

Hall, D. (1989) 'Understanding parents', in Johnson, D. A., Uttley, D. and Wyke, M. (eds) *Children's Head Injury: Who Cares?* London: Taylor & Francis, pp. 171–82.

Hanna-Pladdy, B., Berry, Z. M., Bennett, T., Phillips, H. L. and Gouvier, W. D. (2001) 'Stress as a diagnostic challenge for postconcussive symptoms: sequelae of mild traumatic brain injury or physiological stress response' *Clinical Neuropsychology* 15(3), 289–304.

Hawley, C. A., Ward, A. B., Magnay, A. R. and Long, J. (2003) 'Parental stress and burden following traumatic brain injury amongst children and adolescents', *Brain Injury*, 17(1), 1–23.

Hindley, P. and Reed, H. (1999) 'Promoting Alternative Thinking Strategies (PATHS): mental health promotion with deaf children in school', in Decker, S., Kirby, S., Greenwood, A. and Moore, D. (eds) *Taking Children Seriously.* London: Cassell, pp. 113–30.

Johnson, D. A. (1992) 'Head injured children and education: a need for greater delineation and understanding', *British Journal of Educational Psychology* 62, 404–9.

Kehle, T. J., Clark, E. *et al.* (1997) Interventions for students with traumatic brain injury: managing behavioral disturbances', in Bigler, E., Clark, E. and Farmer, J. (eds) *Childhood Traumatic Brain Injury.* Austin, TX: Pro-Ed, pp. 135–52.

Lehr, E. (1990) *Psychological Management of Traumatic Brain Injuries in Children and Adolescents.* Gaithersburg, MD: Aspen Publishers.

Lehr, E. (1997) 'Counseling students with ABI', in Glang, A., Singer, G. and Todis, B. (eds) *Students with Acquired Brain Injury: The School's Response.* Baltimore, MD: Paul H. Brookes, pp. 277–92.

McCrea, M., Guskiewicz, K. M., Marshall, S. W., Barr, W., Randolph, C., Cantu, R. C., Onate, J. A., Yang, J. and Kelly, J. P. (2003) 'Acute effects and recovery time following concussion in collegiate football players: the NCAA concussion study', *JAMA*, 290(19), 2556–63.

Malkmus, P. and Stenderup, K. (1974) *Levels of Cognitive Functioning.* Downey, CA: Rancho Los Amigos Hospital, Communications Disorders Service.

Mathias, J. L., Beall, J. A. and Bigler, E. D. (2004) 'Neuropsychological and information processing deficits following mild traumatic brain injury.', *Journal of the International Neuropsychological Society*, 10(2), 286–97.

Max, J. E., Castillo, C. S., Robin, D. A., Lindgren, S. D., Smith, W. L., Sato, Y. and Arndt, S. (1998) 'Posttraumatic stress symptomology after childhood traumatic brain injury', *Journal of Nervous & Mental Disease*, 186(10), 589–96.

Middleton, J. (2000) 'Applications in child mental health', *The Psychologist*, 13(1), 27–9.

Mira, M. P., Tucker, B. F. and Tyler, J. S. (1992) *Traumatic Brain Injury in Children and Adolescents: A Sourcebook for Teachers and Other School Personnel.* Austin, TX: Pro-Ed

Mosley, J. (1999) *More Quality Circle Time.* Cambridge: LDA.

Pavri, S. (2001) 'Loneliness in children with disabilities: how can teachers help?', *Teaching Exceptional Children*, 33(6), 52–8.

Pearpoint, J., Forest, M. and O'Brien, J. (1996) 'MAPs, Circles of Friends, and PATH', in Stainback, S. and Stainback, W. (eds) *Inclusion: A Guide for Educators.* Baltimore, MD: Paul H. Brookes, pp. 67–86.

Ponsford, J., Willmott, C., Rothwell, A., Cameron, P., Ayton, G., Nelms, R., Curran, C. and Ng, K. (2001) 'Impact of early intervention on outcome after mild traumatic brain injury in children', *Paediatrics*, 108(6), 1297–303.

Powell, T. (1994) *Head Injury – A Practical Guide.* Nottingham: Headway National Head Injuries Association Ltd (2nd edn published 2001, Bicester: Winslow).

Rappaport, M., Hall, K. M., Hopkins, H. K., *et al.* (1982) 'Disability rating scale for severe head trauma: coma to community', *Archives of Physical Medicine and Rehabilitation,* 63, 118–23.

Royal College of Surgeons of England (1999) *Report of the Working Party in the Management of Patients with Head Injuries.* London: The Royal College of Surgeons of England.

Savage, R. C. (1994) 'An Educator's Guide to the Brain and Brain Injury', in Savage, R. C. and Wolcott, G. F. (eds) *Educational Dimensions of Acquired Brain Injury.* Austin, TX: Pro-Ed, pp. 13–31.

Savage, R. C. (1999) *The Child's Brain: Injury and Development.* Wake Forest, NC: Lash and Associates Publishing/Training Inc.

Savage, R. C. and Morales, K. J. (1996) 'The roller coaster: the changing roles of the family in the ongoing recovery of their child', in Singer, G. H. S., Glang, A. and Williams, J. M. (eds) *Children with Acquired Brain Injury: Educating and Supporting Families,* Baltimore, MD: Paul H. Brookes, pp. 65–78.

Savage, R. C. and Pearson, S. (1997) 'Common questions when serving students with ABI', in Glang, A., Singer, G. and Todis, B. (eds) *Students with Acquired Brain Injury-The School's Response.* Baltimore, MD: Paul H. Brookes, pp. 369–84.

Savage, R., Pearson, S., McDonald, H., Potoczny-Gray, A. and Marchese, N. (2001) 'After hospital: working with schools and families to support the long term needs of children with brain injuries', *Neurorehabilitation,* 16, 49–58.

Savage, R. C. and Wolcott, G. F. (1995) *An Educator's Manual,* Washington, DC: Brain Injury Association, Inc.

Semrud-Clikeman, M. (2001) *Traumatic Brain Injury in Children and Adolescents.* New York: Guilford Press.

Sharples, P. M., Storey, A., Aynsley-Green, A. and Eyre, J. A. (1990) 'Avoidable factors contributing to the death of children with head injury', *British Medical Journal,* 300, 87–9.

Singer, G. H. S. and Nixon, C. (1996) 'A report on the concerns of parents of children with ABI', in Singer, G. H. S., Glang, A. and Williams, J. M. (eds) *Children with Acquired Brain Injury: Educating and Supporting Families,* Baltimore, MD: Paul H. Brookes, pp. 23–52.

Smith, A. (2002) *The Brain's Behind It.* Stafford: Network Educational Press.

Sousa, D. A. (2001) *How the Special Needs Brain Learns.* Thousand Oaks, CA: Corwin Press.

Sternberg, R. J. and Grigorenko, E. (2002) *Dynamic Testing: The Nature and Measurement of Learning Potential.* Cambridge: Cambridge University Press.

Taylor, H. G., Yeates, K. O., Wade, S. L., Drotar, D., Stancin, T. and Minich, N. (2002) 'A prospective study of short- and long-term outcomes after traumatic brain injury in children: behavior and achievement', *Neuropsychology,* 16, 15–27.

Teasdale, G. and Jennet, B. (1974) 'Assessment of coma and impaired consciousness: a practical scale', *Lancet*, 2(872), 81–4.

Tucker, B. F. and Colson, S. E. (1992) 'Traumatic brain injury: an overview of school re-entry', *Intervention in School and Clinic*, 27(4), 198–206.

Tzuriel, D. (2001) *Dynamic Assessment of Young Children.* New York: Plenum Press.

Wolcott, G., Lash, M. and Pearson, S. (1995) *Signs and Strategies for Educating Students with Brain Injuries.* Houston, TX: HDI.

Ylvisaker, M. (ed.) (1998) *Traumatic Brain Injury Rehabilitation – Children and Adolescents*, 2nd edn. Boston, MA: Butterworth-Heinemann.

Ylvisaker, M. and Feeney, T. (1998) *Collaborative Brain Injury Intervention*, San Diego, CA: Singular Publishing Group, Inc.

Ylvisaker, M. and Gioia, G. (1998) 'Cognitive assessment', in Ylvisaker, M. (ed.) *Traumatic Brain Injury Rehabilitation – Children and Adolescents*, 2nd edn. Boston, MA: Butterworth-Heinemann, pp. 159–80.

Ylvisaker, M., Hartwick, P., Ross, B. and Nussbaum, N. (1994) 'Cognitive assessment', in Savage, R. and Wolcott, G. (eds) *Educational Dimensions of Acquired Brain Injury.* Austin, TX: Pro-Ed, pp. 69–120.

Ylvisaker, M., Hartwick, P. and Stevens, M. (1991) 'School re-entry following head injury: managing the transition from hospital to school', *Journal of Head Trauma Rehabilitation*, 6(1),10–22.

Ylvisaker, M. and Szekeres, S. F. (1998) 'A framework for cognitive rehabilitation', in Ylvisaker, M. (ed.) *Traumatic Brain Injury Rehabilitation – Children and Adolescents*, 2nd edn. Boston, MA: Butterworth-Heinemann, pp. 125–58.

Index